New Zealand
in Colour

By the same authors:

Michael King:

Moko: Maori Tattooing in the Twentieth Century
Make It News: How to Approach the Media
Te Ao Hurihuri (ed.)
Tihe Mauri Ora (ed.)
Te Puea
New Zealand: Its Land and its People
New Zealanders at War
The Collector: A Biography of Andreas Reischek

Martin Barriball:

New Zealand: Images, Impressions
The Mobil Illustrated Guide to New Zealand (with Jeremy and Diana Pope)
The North Island in Colour (with Mervyn Dykes)
The South Island in Colour (with Mervyn Dykes)

New Zealand in Colour

Text Michael King

Photographs Martin Barriball

REED

First published 1982

Reprinted 1983

A.H. & A.W. REED LTD
68-74 Kingsford-Smith Street,
Wellington 3
also
7 Kirk Street, Auckland 2
85 Thackeray Street, Christchurch 2

ISBN 0 589 01402 1

Typeset by Jacobson Typesetters Ltd.

Printed by Everbest Printing Co Ltd,
Hong Kong

Contents

Introduction

To the Europeans who rediscovered and settled it, New Zealand was a beautiful but alien land. The recurring note was struck by Abel Tasman. In 1642 the Dutchman became the first known non-Polynesian navigator to sight the country. His sailors clashed with Maoris at Golden Bay after a misunderstanding about trumpet playing (Tasman believed a Maori challenge to fight was simply a display of musical prowess, and he answered it); four seamen were killed. Tasman then sailed the length of the North Island's west coast without landing, seeing only sand dunes and the likelihood of further hostile receptions. He left New Zealand convinced that the country was an inhospitable desert peopled by violent savages.

James Cook did something to redress the balance in the eighteenth century. He found lush harbours and befriended the inhabitants, and his charting of the coast and detailed journal observations led to British colonisation in the nineteenth century. But it still took a long time for European migrants to feel at home in the Antipodes. Most came from the British Isles — from England, Scotland and Ireland. Unlike the handful of continental Europeans, the British were neither drawn nor exalted by mountainous parts of the country. They sought landscapes that seemed most like Britain. And they enhanced the similarity by planting exotic trees and flowers, by introducing English birds, and by constructing English-looking churches and cottages. They tried to transplant what was familiar to them as a means of insulating themselves from what was unfamiliar and therefore frightening.

Right up to the 1950s New Zealand school children learnt a poem that began, "Land of the moa and Maori, land of the kowhai and kauri" — as if these features were strange in the country of their origin. And a nationally recognised poet spoke of "what great gloom stands in a land of settlers with never a soul at home".

The result was that New Zealand became far more than a land of extraordinarily varied landscape. Within that landscape vegetation, fauna and mixed architectural styles created still further diversity. Untamed South Island lakes, backdropped by mountains and virgin forest, contrast with manicured city ones featuring stately willows and white swans. Sections of highway bounded by rimu, kahikatea and kowhai are succeeded by others lined with rhododendrons and camelias. Pastureland is as likely to be dotted with poplars and macrocarpa as it is with cabbage tree and ponga. Rivers surge mightily from rock gorges and meander elsewhere through daffodil-lined banks. And throughout the country native fantails, tui and silvereyes compete in gardens with blackbirds, thrushes and sparrows. Flora, fauna and landscape are every bit as thoroughly colonised and variegated as the country's inhabitants.

The native Maori population has been the constant witness to these changes. Arriving in New Zealand more than 1,200 years ago, Maoris were always more intimately at home there than later migrants. They necessarily lived closer to the land and its seasons because they brought so little with them in canoe voyages. They depended on wild roots, on birds, on fish and shellfish, on some cultivated crops, and on the wood and stone that were the basis for their material culture and the media for their increasingly complex artistic expression.

Being neolithic and illiterate they carried with them only language, traditions, a few vegetables, some stone and wooden tools, a species of dog and the Polynesian rat. Everything else and everything subsequent that was life-sustaining they had to take from the New Zealand soil. Even their traditions became New Zealand-centred as they made the rapid transition from migrants to tangata whenua, people of the land.

When Europeans appeared the Maori experimented with successive modes of rejection, welcome, further rejection, and finally a reluctant and then a confident compromise with the culture and technology of the new colonists. Their numbers plummeted close to extinction in the late nineteenth century and then rose sharply in the twentieth as they acquired immunity from European diseases and strengthened Maori cultural roots by a controlled accommodation of Western culture. They remain a constant reminder that New Zealand is a Pacific rather than a European nation — in the meeting houses and pa scattered over the North Island, in the literal colour of the Polynesian faces, and in the proverbial colour which Maori values and customs bring to the nation's more staid Anglo-Saxon habits. As a component of the national life the Maori element now waxes rather than wanes.

Up to and immediately after World War II Europeans in New Zealand still referred to England as "home". It took them a long time to feel that they and the fauna they brought with them belonged in the new country. Since the 1940s their numbers have been swollen further by immigrants from countries such as Greece, Poland, Holland, India, China and Cambodia, and from the Pacific Islands.

By the 1980s, Pakeha — the Maori word for stranger — had ceased to mean "outsider". It now refers simply to non-Polynesian New Zealanders. The components of population remain as diverse as the landscape. But they have ceased to look abroad for identity and inspiration; they now find these things confidently within the borders of their own country. And the literature which used to express disquiet and remoteness from cultural origins now celebrates a nation at home with itself and its own people, Maori and Pakeha.

CAPE REINGA LIGHTHOUSE

The Far North

The Far North

The Far North is in every sense the cradle of European culture in New Zealand — and possibly of Maori culture, too, although this is more difficult to establish. Certainly Maoris were settled in Northland 1,100 years ago, and the earliest traces of agriculture in the country have been found there, in the Bay of Islands. Some scholars are convinced it was the first part of New Zealand to be colonised by Polynesians. They suggest that the canoe migration myths, which most Maori tribes retain, refer not to an ocean journey to New Zealand but to major movements of population out of Northland to southern parts of the country. Today the Ngapuhi, Te Aupouri, Te Rarawa, Te Mahurehure and Ngati Whatua tribes make up a sizable and energetic section of the region's population. They are concentrated mainly in the northern counties, and the most visible signs of their presence are the

marae and meeting houses (many not carved) dotted across the landscape.

Europeans were drawn to Northland in the late eighteenth century. Traders, whalers and adventurers homed in on the Bay of Islands as a major South Pacific port. It gained a reputation for lawlessness and violence. On the west coast Hokianga Harbour also attracted ships seeking shelter, spars and provisions. Incidents such as the burning of the ship *Boyd* by Maoris in Whangaroa Harbour in 1809 brought a degree of notoriety to New Zealand.

In 1814 an Anglican missionary, Samuel Marsden of Sydney, preached to Maoris for the first time and later established a mission at the Bay of Islands. Other denominations — especially Wesleyans and Roman Catholics — followed and also began their evangelising in the Far North. With them they brought agriculture and literacy, believing that their task was to civilise the Maoris in addition to saving their souls.

The Bay of Islands also became the country's first administrative centre. A British Resident, James Busby, was appointed in 1833 to see to the interests of British subjects, and it was largely as a consequence of his reports that the colony's first Lieutenant-Governor, Captain William Hobson, arrived there in 1840 to effect a treaty with the Maoris. The Treaty of Waitangi was carried throughout the country, but was initially signed in front of Busby's residence in the Bay of Islands. It offered the natives the protection of the British Crown in return for their ceding the sovereignty of the country to Queen Victoria. It led to the annexation of New Zealand by Britain the same year, and to the establishment of the colony's first capital near Kororareka, the present township of Russell.

From the 1840s the economic and administrative importance of Northland declined. The capital was transferred to Auckland. There was a boom in kauri timber and kauri gum, but both were ruthlessly exploited and depleted. Northland diminished in national importance and its quiet communities — with the exception of Whangarei — now attract tourists rather than investment capital.

1. Cape Reinga was known to the Maori as Te Rerenga Wairua — the place where the spirits of the dead leap into the Underworld. Beyond it lies Cape Maria van Diemen, named in 1642 by the Dutch navigator Abel Tasman after the wife of his sponsor.

2. Buses drive up Northland's Ninety Mile Beach and stop to allow passengers to stroll on its open sands.

3. To the east, Whangaroa Harbour's hills provide both an ideal anchorage for small craft and shelter for holiday cottages.

3

1

2

1. Russell, known formerly as Kororareka, is close to the site of the country's first capital. It was a favourite port for whalers and adventurers from the late 1700s. According to one writer, the orgies there were "such as would defile the pages of history". New Zealand's first Vice-Regal representative, Captain William Hobson, set up his capital at nearby Okiato in 1840, and a Union Jack was flown from the hill above Russell township. In 1844 a war in the north was precipitated when a Ngapuhi chief dissatisfied with British rule chopped down the flagstaff. Fighting followed between Maori and British Imperial troops. In 1845 the flagstaff was cut down twice more, and in March of that year Russell was sacked and burnt with a loss of 13 European lives. The dissident Maoris were finally defeated at Ruapekapeka in January 1846. The residents of Russell returned and rebuilt their township. Now it is the administrative and holiday centre for the Bay of Islands. In particular it acts as a base for the district's popular big-game fishing, which includes marlin and shark admired throughout the world for their magnitude. Russell is also the point of departure for sight-seeing and other fishing trips around the harbour. It is linked by launch services to Paihia and Opua across the bay.

2. Piercy Island off Cape Brett in the Bay of Islands has a famous hole in the rock through which boats can sail. In naming it after Admiralty official Sir Piercy Brett, Captain James Cook was also enjoying a pun.

1

2

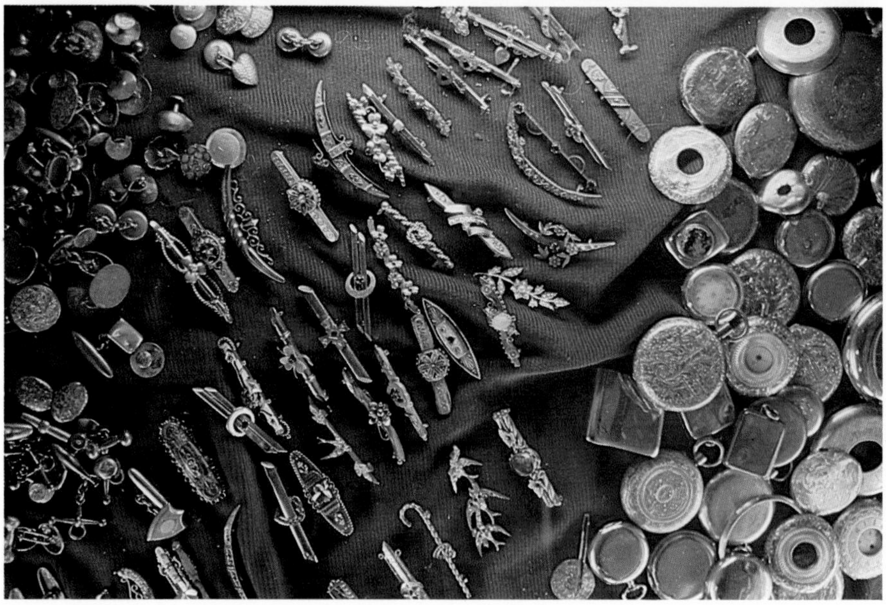

3

1. A unique feature of the Bay of Islands is Kelly Tarlton's Shipwreck Museum on board the barque *Tui* at Paihia. Underwater archaeology did not exist in New Zealand until Tarlton and his friend Wade Doak began to look for and explore New Zealand wrecks in the 1960s.

2. Exhibits include pieces of ships, maritime equipment, jewellery (including relics of the Rothschild Collection) and some of the first wrist watches.

3. A special feature of the collection is gold jewellery and coins salvaged from the *Elingamite* and *Tasmania* wrecks. The *Elingamite*, object of Tarlton's first major expedition, ran on to rocks and sank off the Three Kings Islands in November 1902. Forty-five people drowned in the disaster. Tarlton and Doak recovered a large number of coins from the ship's submerged skeleton. The *Tasmania* went down off Mahia Peninsula in 1897 with a loss of 13 lives. In the case of both wrecks, a large part of their interest lay in the discovery of passengers' personal effects.

4

4. Kerikeri Inlet on the northern side of the Bay of Islands is a fine anchorage. It is the site of the second Anglican mission station in the country, established there in 1819. Opposite the mission settlement stood Kororipo, home pa of the notorious Ngapuhi fighting chief Hongi Hika. Hongi visited England and Australia in 1820 and 1821 and returned to Kerikeri with over 1,000 muskets. He armed his warriors with them and went south to subjugate the tribes of the North Island. He was largely successful because his adversaries had not acquired muskets.

5. Kerikeri today is the centre of New Zealand's largest citrus-growing area. The old stone store, built in 1833, is now a museum. Next to it is the country's oldest building, the Kemp homestead, built for the mission in 1819. The following year the Anglicans there introduced the plough to New Zealand.

5

1

2

1-3. Maori costume is most likely to be seen nowadays on ceremonial occasions: headbands, sashes and piupiu (flax skirts) for the men; these and bodices for the women. Most of the woven material is decorated with colourful taniko patterns. On such occasions — and this one commemorates the signing of the Treaty of Waitangi in February 1840 — Maoris provide challenges, haka (posture dances) and action songs. The men are loud, aggressive performers; the women specialise in soft lilting music, often accompanied by hand and arm movements or by actions with the traditional poi. Without contributions of this kind New Zealand would be largely devoid of colourful ceremony. At Waitangi Day celebrations Maoris are joined by sailors of the Royal New Zealand Navy, who complement Polynesian grace with their own more disciplined formations.

3

4. The Maori meeting house at Waitangi is unusual in that its carvings represent the ancestors and designs of all Maori tribes, not simply those of the local Ngapuhi. These panels were carved in the 1930s by a team from all over the country. The meeting house itself was intended as a national marae or forum, emphasising the respect with which Maoris hold Waitangi as the place where their ancestors solemnly ceded the sovereignty of the country to the British Crown. While some have questioned the validity of the treaty in subsequent years, the majority still regard it as the symbol and cornerstone of Maori–Pakeha co-operation.

5. Another Maori site close to Waitangi is Rewa's model village near Kerikeri, named after Hongi Hika's second-in-command. This complex is a re-creation of a pre-European pa with fortifications, palisades, huts, a storehouse and a chief's dwelling. All are made from traditional materials and to traditional designs.

6. The site where the Treaty of Waitangi was first signed is now part of a national memorial. The ceremony took place in front of James Busby's house, known today simply as the Treaty House. Built in the early 1830s it is a fine example of early colonial architecture. Busby is less well known as New Zealand's first grape grower and wine maker — a tradition that was not to flourish in New Zealand until well into the twentieth century. The house itself was bought by a much-loved Governor-General of New Zealand, Lord Bledisloe, and he donated it to the nation in 1932. It is now the scene of the annual Waitangi Day celebrations and draws thousands of visitors at other times of the year.

4

5

6

1

2

1. Tairua Bay is typical of dozens of sheltered beaches on Northland's east coast. The white sand and quiet blue water fringed by pohutukawa trees and toetoe are characteristic of the area and have made it immensely popular with holiday makers, campers and real-estate agents. All this is in contrast to Northland's west coast. That too has a beauty of its own, but of a far more rugged variety. The open beaches have high dunes, and surf pounds in dangerously. The harbours tend to be muddy and edged with mangroves. The result is that the demand for property and facilities has been higher on the east coast, and the west is less developed and less populous.

2. Inland Northland also holds surprises. The Whangarei Falls close to Whangarei city are set in seven hectares of bush and drop 24 metres into a wide and tree-lined basin. They are one of several tourist targets in the area. Others include the high bluffs of Bream Head at the entrance to Whangarei Harbour, and Kamo Springs to the north of the city.

3. Northland's sub-tropical climate supports many plants that are less likely to grow in other parts of the country. One is the hibiscus, which grows prolifically in gardens throughout the district. Some people have even succeeded in cultivating bananas and pineapples, though not in commercial quantities. Millions of years ago the Far North also supported a New Zealand coconut palm. Although it has long since disappeared as a result of climatic changes, fossilised coconuts with three holes at the base occasionally wash up on Northland beaches.

4. In Northland, as elsewhere throughout the country, wading birds flourish in rivers, swamps and estuaries. One of the most versatile and most graceful is the pied stilt, which enjoys all three environments and is often seen on inland waterways. This one is immature. When it is fully grown its plumage will settle into more sharply contrasting black and white.

3

Auckland

Auckland

Auckland — known as the Queen City — prides itself on being the country's most elegant metropolis, and its most hedonistic one. Its establishment dates from Lieutenant-Governor Hobson's decision to take the capital there in 1841. It retained this status until 1865, a major factor in its early growth. In Hobson's vision it was an ideal site. It lay on an isthmus between two large and sheltered harbours, and because most of the country's trading activities then centred on the northern part of the country, it was close to areas of economic importance. In addition Maori settlement on the isthmus — although it had once been extensive — was thin by 1841. And so Hobson bought the site of the town from the Ngati Whatua owners.

The wisdom of the decision was confirmed by subsequent events, even though the capital eventually went to Wellington. After a brief gold and

2

agricultural boom in the South Island later in the century, Auckland regained and held the commercial initiative for much of the twentieth century. It has remained the country's largest and most prosperous city. Its industries thrive, its ports continue to ship out agricultural produce and manufactured goods, and to import those items which the country is unable to make itself. Equally important, Auckland's climate and room for unlimited growth have pulled in residents and businesses in large numbers.

The range of lifestyle options which the city offers are important to Aucklanders and to visitors alike. There are two harbours on the city doorstep and four more within a couple of hours' drive. The Hauraki Gulf, protected by the Coromandel Peninsula, offers the safest large area of water in the country for boating and fishing. There are dozens of beaches and bush reserves within easy distance. Auckland is also better endowed with parks — especially the Domain and Cornwall Park — than any other New Zealand community. In summer Aucklanders turn out *en masse* for outdoor recreation — walking, swimming, yachting, fishing. The city is the most outdoor-oriented in the country. It is not surprising, perhaps, that the phenomenon of jogging has caught on here so strongly. The sport's popularity has increased to such an extent that the annual Round the Bays run attracts a crowd of over 80,000, from primary-school children to octogenarians.

Aucklanders are proud of their city, its facilities and its achievements. Its suburbs are the most extensive in the country, and many of them are also the most picturesque, especially those overlooking the sea. The inner city, especially Ponsonby and Herne Bay, is undergoing a renewal and becoming a focal point of the city's nightlife. All this makes them confident, even — sometimes — boastful. But they have much to boast about.

1. Like a great coathanger the harbour bridge links Auckland's North Shore and city. People who once lived hours away from Queen Street can now commute to the heart of town in 10 minutes. High-rise offices in the background are the imprimatur of success shared by prosperous cities the world over.

2. Pohutukawa are among Auckland's most treasured assets. The waterfront drive — here at Kohimarama, and elsewhere — is lined with them. Flowering in December they fully live up to their reputation as the country's own Christmas trees.

3. Mission Bay at summer's height is crammed with sunbathers of all ages. Aucklanders are above all else a beach people.

3

22
30

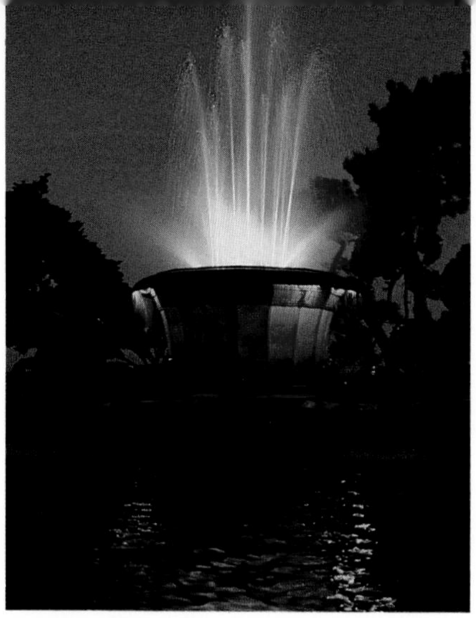

2

1. Auckland may no longer be the nation's political capital, but it is certainly the yachting capital. More money is spent on boats here than in the rest of the country put together; here too competitions are more numerous and more intense. It is a long-established tradition that brings out yachts in their thousands on the annual Anniversary Day Regatta in January.

2. The Mission Bay fountain flares spectacularly in the dark, one of the gems of Auckland's nightlife.

3. Jogging, which has developed into a national sport, began in Auckland. This happened largely because of the world-famous exploits of local athletes such as Arthur Lydiard, Murray Halberg and Peter Snell. Now joggers are to be seen everywhere in the city at all times of the year — here in Mission Bay or on other beaches, in the city's many parks, or simply along pavements.

4. The sheltered nature of the Hauraki Gulf, its dozens of islands and hundreds of safe beaches, ensures that a considerable proportion of Auckland's resources is tied up in large yachts and launches. This marina at Half Moon Bay on the Tamaki Inlet is only one of many jammed with expensive craft.

5. Waiheke Island is the third largest in the country, discounting the mainland. It is surrounded by idyllic beaches with exotic names such as Palm Beach (shown here, on the island's eastern side), Blackpool, Cowes, Surfdale and Ostend. In addition to holiday makers the island has a large permanent population.

3

4

5

1

2

1. Rangitoto Island, Auckland Harbour and sunrise from Okahu Bay, Orakei. Although the city is built on a chain of volcanoes, Rangitoto is the only one to have erupted within the period of human occupation. Maoris gave it the name, which means "bleeding skies", as a result of witnessing its convulsions. Several Maori villages were buried under its ash, including one on adjacent Motutapu Island. Okahu Bay, now an anchorage for large yachts, was for a long time the refuge of the remnants of the Ngati Whatua tribe, from whom Lieutenant-Governor William Hobson bought the site of Auckland city. The tribe clung to a steadily shrinking pa here until the early 1950s, when members were persuaded to move on to the hill overlooking the bay. On the flat, however, they left their burial ground and a small chapel, the last relics of the old settlement.

2. St Stephen's Church at Judges Bay in Parnell is one of the city's oldest links with its past. Built in 1857, it broods over a fragment of the harbour foreshore which has been kept as it was a century ago. Beyond the grass, the graves and the beach, however, the main trunk railway line, Tamaki Drive and the port's container terminal remind the browser that Auckland has moved far and fast in the limited period of Pakeha settlement.

Provincial North Island

Provincial North Island

Provincial North Island is in every sense the backbone of New Zealand. Its landscape contains every feature that characterises the country as a whole, barring the Southern Alps: snow-capped peaks, bush-clad ranges, a desert plateau, a volcanic crust and thermal activity, sprawling lakes, meandering rivers, rolling hill country, flat pastureland and every possible variety of coastline. The scenery may not be as arresting as that in the alpine south, but it is typical of most of New Zealand.

The same could be said of the people. The population of large centres such as Hamilton, New Plymouth, Wanganui and Gisborne are — literally and metaphorically — middle New Zealand. They preach and practise the virtues of provincial life: hard work, respect for and reliance on primary industry, a strong emphasis on private enterprise and individual rights, a commitment to rugby and

horse racing, and a conservative political orientation. In the smaller rural towns such as Taumarunui, Hawera and Pahiatua, these qualities are even more pronounced. In particular the city visitor is likely to be reminded forcefully that 80 per cent of New Zealand's export income still derives from agriculture. And the dairy farms, sheep runs and cattle stations of the rural North Island are responsible for generating most of it.

Some parts of the island have also come to rely increasingly on tourism for income. The New Zealander's 40-hour week and tradition of paid holidays allows considerable movement within the country, and the age of the jumbo jet is bringing tourists from abroad at the rate of over 300,000 a year (mainly from the United States, Australia, Canada and Japan).

The major area that beckons holiday seekers is the central North Island: Rotorua with its thermal novelties and strongly visible manifestations of Maori culture, and Taupo with trout fishing in its lake and rivers, especially the Tongariro. Other areas, too, have much to offer. The Waitomo Caves provide the most spectacular accessible examples of stalagmites and stalactites in the country. The skiing on Mt Ruapehu's Whakapapa and Turoa fields is admirable. Other mountains and ranges, especially Egmont, provide challenging climbs. The Urewera National Park boasts the largest area of virgin bush in the island and endless opportunities for camping, tramping, fishing and deer stalking. Beach resorts swell in popularity, particularly the sun-drenched shores of the Bay of Plenty and the extraordinary variety of the Coromandel Peninsula.

Provincial North Island also houses the majority of the country's rural Maori population. Although most Maoris now live in cities alongside the Pakeha, it is in country communities that Maori values and institutions — especially those of the marae — are strongest: places such as Ngaruawahia, Ruatoria and Tokaanu, to name a few. These keep the traditional bases for the culture strong and vital.

1. The beach at Whangaroa on the East Cape has a characteristically rugged shore which thrusts into the sea at the country's furthest point east.

2. At the Ruakura Research Centre in Hamilton animals and pasture are under constant study. Funded by the Government, scientists here look for new ways of increasing the efficiency and the output of primary production in New Zealand.

3. Mt Tarawera, brooding over the lake of the same name, was the last New Zealand volcano to erupt on a major scale, in 1886. Today it dominates a landscape that it once devastated with lava and ash.

3

1

2

3

1. The township of Coromandel was a "boom and bust" community. Like the peninsula on which it stands, it was named after the British warship *Coromandel* which called into its harbour for kauri spars in 1820. That visit set the pattern for future development. The settlement swelled in the 1850s as a port from which much Coromandel timber, especially kauri, was shipped out to Auckland and Australia.

In 1852 a sawmiller named Charles Ring discovered gold-bearing quartz close to the township. He rushed at once to Auckland to claim the Provincial Government's £250 prize for the finder of the first "payable" goldfield. This had been offered in an effort to check the drift of population away from the province to the Australian and Californian goldfields. Ring's discovery triggered New Zealand's first gold rush at Coromandel. Forty-two square kilometres around the harbour were leased from Maori owners and the search began. It petered out, however, when it was discovered that the ore could be extracted only by employing expensive machinery.

A second rush in the area in the 1860s proved more lasting and more lucrative. Coromandel and Thames were the centres and both waxed large on prospectors' money. By the 1880s it was all over, however, and the miners and prospectors drifted away or turned their attention to milling or gum digging. Coromandel retains several fine buildings erected during the rush, especially the Gold Warden's Court, which now serves as the County Council chambers. Mine shafts can also been seen around the township, though most are too dangerous to enter.

2. This bay close to Coromandel township is typical of the peninsula's west side. The beaches are more precipitate, tend to mud rather than sand, and look out across the Hauraki Gulf to the South Auckland coast.

3. Wharekaho Beach north of Whitianga lies within the wide sweep of Mercury Bay, the best harbour on the Coromandel Peninsula. The bay was named by James Cook in commemoration of his observation of the transit of Mercury across the sun here in 1769. Cook made careful records of the Maoris and of the settlements in which they lived. It is one of the few areas in the country where archaeology can be linked back to historical records to shed light on how the Maoris lived in pre-European days. The white sand beaches here are typical of those on the east side of the peninsula, which is also more indented than the coast to the west.

Like Coromandel, Mercury Bay prospered initially from the trade in kauri timber and — in its wake — in kauri gum. This gives the area an affinity with Northland. Many individuals and families worked both areas for the same commodities. After the gold rushes the peninsula was found to be rich in other minerals, and this has made it a favourite target for gemstone collectors.

1

2

3

1. Like many seaside communities in the Bay of Plenty Mt Maunganui has a small permanent population that swells by thousands during the summer months as city dwellers head for the coast. It is one of the country's most popular resorts, close to Tauranga city and recognisable from afar by the sugarloaf hill that gives the beach its name.

2. Terns are among New Zealand's most common and most appealing seabirds. Less numerous and decidedly more graceful than the scavenging gulls, they fly in small flocks in search of schools of fish. When they find their prey they fall on them from the sky with unerring accuracy.

3. Hamilton is New Zealand's fourth largest city. It stands on the banks of the Waikato River, the country's largest waterway. Founded by Imperial soldiers in 1864, it was built on the site of a Maori village and group of cultivations known as Kirikiriroa. The Maori inhabitants were driven off as a result of the Waikato War of that year and the subsequent confiscation by the Government of a million acres (405,000 hectares) of their land. The area confiscated turned out to be the richest dairy pastureland in the country. Hamilton grew up largely servicing this new industry. From the mid-twentieth century it became progressively more industrialised and spread its basis of prosperity. It remains more than anything else a river city, and a garden city. The banks of the Waikato have been kept largely in parkland close to the business area and residents and visitors take advantage of this civic asset. Four bridges span the river to link the east bank with the commercial area.

4. In recent years the more torrential North Island rivers — previously not regarded as navigable — have found new popularity as wilderness areas for rafting. Enthusiasts take to the waters to shoot rapids in rubber dinghies. Helmets and lifejackets ensure that accidents are kept to a minimum. This group negotiates the Wairoa River near Tauranga.

4

1. Maori tribes in the centre of the North Island were well known in the nineteenth century for their craftsmanship on water. Lakes and rivers served as a means of transport, a source of food and as a protection against surprise attack. But for the Arawa people, whose headquarters were on Mokoia Island in Lake Rotorua, the lake's waters were insufficient protection against muskets. When Hongi Hika of Ngapuhi swept through here in 1823 he killed 3,000 of them.

2, 3. The best-known river tribes were those of the Waikato. They patrolled their territory by canoe and made war from these craft. During the Waikato War, however, most canoes were broken up by Imperial troops. Seventy years later a leader called Princess Te Puea Herangi revived canoe building as part of her efforts to restore the morale of Waikato Maoris. Although the vessels were never again used for fighting, extensive use is made of them on ceremonial occasions. One of the most popular is the annual Ngaruawahia regatta, held close to Turangawaewae Marae, centre of the Maori King Movement. Here canoes and canoists go through their paces, the participants dressed in traditional costume and using traditional instruments.

1

2

3

4

5

4, 5. In the 1870s the district around Lake Rotorua became New Zealand's first major tourist attraction. What drew visitors from home and abroad was the combination of lakes and springs, living Maori culture and thermal marvels. It was the last of these that evoked most interest. The Rotorua section of the central North Island plateau sits on a cauldron of volcanic activity. In places the ground lid is relatively thin and this activity breaks through in the form of hot springs, geysers or boiling mud pools. The most famous of the geysers used to be Waimangu, which blew itself out in 1917. The best-known now is Pohutu at Whakarewarewa on the outskirts of Rotorua city, which rises over 30 metres. Boiling mud is also a source of fascination for visitors to "Whaka". The process by which it inflates thick bubbles which finally burst and push out concentric circles is reminiscent of simmering porridge. The other attractive feature of the region is the texture of rocks and terraces in the thermal areas, many of them composed of colourful silica. The most famous of these formations were the Pink and White Terraces above Lake Rotomahana, which disappeared in the Tarawera eruption of 1886.

6. Whakarewarewa is also of interest for its close association with Maori culture. Its thermal area is owned by a sub-tribe of the Arawa federation who live there still, sometimes cooking meat and vegetables in boiling pools. Maori guides take visitors around the complex which includes a reconstructed Maori pa with carved posts between the palisades, and an arts and crafts centre.

6

1

2

1. Tudor Towers, which now houses Rotorua's museum and a restaurant, was once an enormous bath house complex run by the Government. At the turn of the century — in the heyday of spa resorts — the Government was deliberating whether Te Aroha on the Hauraki Plains or Rotorua would be given the nod for official support. Rotorua was eventually chosen, largely because of the additional attractions of Maoris and geysers. This began a long period in which Rotorua was made famous for the allegedly restorative powers of its thermal spring waters. People suffering from arthritis, gout, the effects of strokes and a host of other ailments came to Rotorua to "take the cure". The process was a major foundation of the town's growing tourist industry. Today Rotorua's springs are not lauded as extravagantly, and the Government bath house has closed. Tudor Towers has become a complex catering for more conventional tourist needs and bowls are a popular sport with players on the lawns outside.

3

4

2. Rotorua's proximity to half a dozen lakes ensures that visitors get to see a wide selection of waterfowl and other wildlife. Black swans used to thrive in New Zealand but became extinct before the arrival of Europeans, in part because they were hunted by early Maoris. The black swans which now populate the lakes have been introduced from Australia. Native and introduced ducks also congregate in large numbers.

3. Hongi's Track is an exquisite 1.6 kilometre section of road through bush on the Rotorua–Whakatane road. It is named after the Ngapuhi warlord Hongi Hika who cut the track to allow his canoes to be dragged from Lake Rotoehu to Lake Rotoiti. This was in 1823 when he was on his way to attack the Arawa stronghold on Mokoia Island on Lake Rotorua. Previously the area had been known as Te Whakamarura-o-Hinehopu — "the sunshade of Hinehopu". The name had been given in honour of a sixteenth-century Arawa chieftainess who planted a matai tree on the spot where she met her future husband, Pikiao. These two became the progenitors of a major Arawa sub-tribe, Ngati Pikiao. Hinehopu's matai still stands on the track where it is known as "the wishing tree". Travellers are advised by Maori elders to pause under the tree in the course of their journey, to offer a prayer to honour it and to leave a piece of greenery at its base to placate the spirit of the place. Once this is carried out no misfortune will befall the traveller on that trip.

4. South-east of Rotorua stands Kaingaroa, at 150,000 hectares the largest man-made forest in the world. Planting with radiata pine began in 1923, and during the Depression of the 1930s the entire empty Kaingaroa Plains were planted, largely to provide work for the unemployed. The pines mature in about 35 years — two-and-a-half times as fast in New Zealand as in their native California — and are versatile in their use. They now constitute New Zealand's major building material and major timber export.

1

1. The Waimangu ("black water") thermal area is the best-known in the country after Whakarewarewa. It includes the Waimangu Cauldron, a boiling lake that covers more than 10 hectares and is the largest of its kind in the world. The cauldron fills a crater left by a major eruption in 1917 which also blew out the great Waimangu Geyser. Above the lake, wreathed in steam, stand the famous Cathedral Rocks, so named because of their similarity to examples of European gothic architecture. Other attractions in the area include Lake Rotomahana, which was a second crater in the Tarawera eruption of 1886 and which swallowed the Pink and White Terraces, and Ruamoko's Throat, a turquoise lake under scarlet cliffs.

2. The thermal valley at Waiouru was only the second place in the world in which natural steam was successfully harnessed to make electricity. Bores driven deep into the earth capture the steam and pipe it to generators at high temperature and under immense pressure. Water from the adjacent Waikato River is used to condense the steam and intensify pressure, thus creating twice as much electricity as thermal pressure would on its own. The power that results provides about five per cent of the country's requirement. The technology developed by New Zealand in refining this process has

2

since been shared with other countries, particularly in South America. For the visitor to Waiouru the effect of all this is an awesome inferno of noise and smoke that drifts out of the valley and across the main north-south highway.

3, 4. Close to its source at Lake Taupo the mighty Waikato River narrows suddenly to pass through a 15-metre chasm which produces a turbulence of rapids. Below them lie the Huka Falls; above them, nestled into the river bank among protective trees, stands the country's best-known fishing lodge, Huka Lodge, named after the falls. Built by the legendary fishing guide Alan Pye in the 1930s, the lodge used to cater for the rich and the great from all over the globe: Royalty, General Douglas MacArthur, Charles Lindburgh and Barbara Hutton are just a few of those who stayed and fished there. The Queen Mother caught a three-and-a-half kilogram trout there in 1958. Derelict in the 1970s, the lodge was taken over by new proprietors who have given it a reputation for superb gourmet cooking, specialising in game food. Huka Falls themselves are a spectacular spurt of turquoise water. The name, appropriately enough, is from the Maori word for foam. A swing bridge allows visitors to cross the river and view the falls from both banks.

3

4

5. The boat harbour at the north-east corner of Lake Taupo is also the lake's major outlet and the beginning of the Waikato River's 354-kilometre run to the sea south of the Manukau Harbour. Maori tribes who lay claim to the river's bed, however, assert that it actually begins in the Tongariro River, south of Lake Taupo. Speaking in terms of strict geography, experts agree. Prior to the Taupo eruption of about A.D.135 the river flowed continuously from the Tongariro bed to its outlet in the Firth of Thames on the opposite side of the coast to its present course.

5

1

1. Looking at Acacia Bay on the western shore of Lake Taupo it requires considerable imagination to recall that the lake is the country's largest volcanic crater. When it erupted some 1,800 years ago, it hurled ash all over the centre of the North Island and left a vast hole, into which flowed the Tongariro River. Thus New Zealand's largest lake was created. When Europeans penetrated the district in 1839 the lake was settled and owned by the Ngati Tuwharetoa tribe, led by the famous line of Te Heuheu chiefs. Tribal traditions state that one of their ancestors named Tia discovered the lake and named it Taupo-nui-a-Tia: "Tia's great shoulder cloak."

2

2. Taupo is best known today as New Zealand's premier fishing resort. Brown trout from Tasmania and rainbow trout from California were introduced in the lake and its feeder rivers in the late nineteenth century. Both varieties adapted spectacularly well to the new conditions. While numbers were low and feed plentiful the fish grew to prodigious size — catches including brown trout over 10 kilograms were not uncommon. Now fish up to four kilograms may be caught more often with the average being about two kilograms. Trolling and casting are both popular and successful on the lake.

3

3. Taranaki Falls are one of the many varied features of the massive Tongariro National Park and are about one hour's walk from the Chateau Tongariro Hotel. They are formed by a stream dropping 25 metres down an old lava flow.

4. Lake Rotoaira lies behind a natural palisade of cabbage trees below the slopes of Mt Tongariro. It is an idyllic scenic spot reached by two separate routes, one from Tokaanu, the other off the main north-south highway. Unlike Lake Taupo, this waterway and its environs still belong to the Ngati Tuwharetoa people and cannot be fished without a special permit.

The Tongariro Power Project, which gathers water from the headwaters of a number of rivers including the Tongariro and the Wanganui, pumps an additional volume through Rotoaira and on to Taupo. The force created generates electricity in a power station at Tokaanu, and also increases the capacity of older stations on the Waikato River by increasing the flow of water through them. During construction for the project, a nineteenth-century pa site on the shore of Rotoaira was excavated to prevent its being damaged by development. The site is now marked on the Tongariro-Tokaanu road and the results of the investigation can be viewed in the project museum at Turangi. The employment of a professional archaeologist as an integral part of the project was an innovation for New Zealand public works schemes and set a precedent for subsequent ones. As the nation matures its citizens are showing increasing respect for its past and a reluctance to lose relics of its heritage.

5. The Tongariro River is the finest stretch of trout water in New Zealand and its reputation has spread among fishermen throughout the world. This view shows the Red Hut Pool, one of dozens of spots sought by those who know the river. Close by is one of the country's four trout hatcheries. It is used primarily for milking ova from rainbow trout. These are fertilised and then nurtured in incubators for about 18 days, by which time the eyes of the fish are visible. A killing-off process eliminates weaker eggs and those that survive — about five million a year — are sent off to rearing stations in other parts of the country and abroad. In this way the major trout-fishing rivers and lakes are kept stocked with fish.

6. Silvereyes, which enjoy nectar from the kowhai tree, are relatively recent immigrants. They introduced themselves from Australia in the mid-nineteenth century and have spread all over New Zealand and its offshore islands.

4

5

6

1

1. The Tongariro National Park was the country's first, a gift to the people of New Zealand from the Ngati Tuwharetoa paramount chief Te Heuheu Tukino IV in 1887. This was only 15 years after Yellowstone Park in the United States had been established as the first such park in the world. The Tongariro park's nucleus was the three volcanic cones that rise so spectacularly and unexpectedly from the desert of the central North Island plateau: Tongariro (1,968 metres), Ngauruhoe (2,290 metres) and Ruapehu (2,796 metres), the last being the highest peak in the North Island. The mountains were sacred places to Ngati Tuwharetoa, who regarded them as repositories of the mana of the tribe and who also used them for burials. The initial bequest extended to a radius of 1.6 kilometres from all three peaks, an area of 2,600 hectares. Later acquisitions by successive governments swelled the park to its current size of 66,600 hectares. Te Heuheu's initial generosity placed the area outside private ownership and potential commercial exploitation, thus protecting much of its tapu in

2

3

Maori eyes. In addition to mountain skiing, the park offers challenging climbs, long walks through bush and tussock, some 500 species of native plants, springs, small lakes and several waterfalls.

2. Mt Ngauruhoe is the most active volcano on the New Zealand mainland. The Tongariro National Park already offers a paradox of desert and snow, and to this Ngauruhoe adds smoke and steam throughout the winter. The steam and gasses are emitted continuously, and every few years a more spectacular eruption throws out ash and sometimes lava. Since World War II the mountain has had two periods of major eruption. With Mt Egmont, Ngauruhoe is one of the most conical mountains in the world and inevitably invites comparison with Mt Fujiama in Japan.

3. Ruapehu is the only other active onshore volcano in New Zealand. It is a far larger and broader peak than Ngauruhoe and carries the best ski slopes in the North Island on its shoulders. One such ski field is the Whakapapa on the Chateau or northern side of the mountain; the other, Turoa, is on the south or Ohakune side. The Chateau is one of the country's best-known luxury hotels. It stands fortress-like at the base of the mountain. Behind it lie the Whakapapa village, the National Park headquarters, and lower-priced accommodation facilities. Further up the slopes at the Top of the Bruce are a profusion of ski-club huts. Higher still a series of chairlifts and rope tows carries skiers up the Whakapapa field.

1

2

1. The Mokau Falls are but one of several arrestingly beautiful waterfalls that descend into Lake Waikaremoana. The lake (whose name means "sea of sparkling water") lies in the centre of the 211,000-hectare Urewera National Park. Surrounded by the largest area of virgin bush in the North Island, it is also regarded as the most attractive lake in the island. The Huiarau Range provides a backdrop to the north while the spectacular Panekiri Bluff rises a sheer 610 metres from the south. Within the bush can be seen virtually every native North Island plant and land bird.

2. So dense is the bush and so difficult the terrain that the Urewera district remained closed to Europeans longer than any other part of New Zealand. The conservative Tuhoe tribe allowed only a small degree of Pakeha contact at the end of the nineteenth century, and even then it was unwilling. It was not until after World Warr II that the Tuhoe people began extensive contact with the rest of the nation.

3

3. The Mokau River inlet is one of six arms to Lake Waikaremoana, all of which support large numbers of waterfowl. Maoris believed that the lake and its inlets were created by the threshings of a taniwha or river monster trapped in its bed.

4. Far to the east of the Urewera National Park the rising sun touches the East Coast of the North Island, lighting it before any other part of the world on that day. The first peak to catch the rays is Mt Hikurangi, which towers above the Maori township of Ruatoria.

1

2

1. New Zealand's native pigeon is the largest and most colourful of the species anywhere in the world.

2. Taranaki's dairy farmland is equalled only by the Waikato in its capacity for production.

3. The peak of Mt Egmont, still called Taranaki by the Maoris, is often wreathed in mist.

3

4. The Wanganui River flows 290 kilometres from its headwaters in the Tongariro National Park to its outlet in the sea near the city of Wanganui. In the North Island it is second only to the Waikato River in length. Before the arrival of Europeans it was an important artery for Maoris to reach the interior of the country by canoe. Settlements sprang up along its bank and many, such as Pipiriki and Jerusalem, were still well populated in the early years of the twentieth century. Europeans too valued the river's opportunity for transport. A steamer service ran for many years from Taumarunui to Wanganui, the whole journey taking three days. Until it ceased in 1934 this route was regarded as one of the country's grandest scenic excursions. With the deterioration of conditions on the upper reaches of the river such transport disappeared, however, and the remaining Maori communities shrank. By the latter part of the twentieth century they were mere shells, and much of the river was reverting to nature.

5. The site of the city of Wanganui was chosen because there are no harbours on the west coast of the North Island between Porirua in the south and Kawhia in the north. the mouth of the Wanganui River was the nearest thing on that coast to an estuary anchorage and provided a convenient stopover between New Plymouth and Wellington. The area was acquired from Maoris by the New Zealand Company as a result of a dubious transaction in 1840. The town was established the same year and grew to become one of the country's quietest and most beautiful provincial centres.

4

5

1. Mahia Peninsula — a large promontory indented with isolated beaches and dotted with holiday cottages — separates Poverty Bay from Hawke's Bay. Many of these beaches boast the clean white sand so popular further up the East Coast and so different from the black ironsand to the west. Poverty Bay to the north was so named by Captain Cook, who made his first New Zealand landfall there in 1769 at Young Nick's Head. Two days later he set foot on New Zealand soil at Kaiti Beach near the present city of Gisborne. There his crew became the first Europeans known to have witnessed a traditional Maori haka or war dance. And when Maoris ran off with sailors' possessions on two successive days there they became the first of their race to be killed by European firearms. Cook designated the area Poverty Bay because, he said, "it afforded us no one thing we wanted."

2. The Waiomoko River runs into the sea at Whangara north of Gisborne. This area is the gateway

1

2

to the East Coast of the North Island, which some commentators have called New Zealand's Riviera. It is a long stretch of shoreline alternating between rocky headlands and richly sanded bays. As coastal scenery it is perhaps equalled only by the Coromandel Peninsula to the north. Unlike Coromandel, however, the Coast (as it is called) is still pleasingly undeveloped. Because much of the land is still in Maori ownership it has escaped the ravages of subdivision and intensive economic development. In part this is a consequence of the complexities of tribal ownership, which makes development difficult even where people want to proceed with it; and in part it results from a conservative unwillingness of Maoris to interfere too drastically with what has been handed down to them by their ancestors. Where Maori farming has been carried on at the Coast, however, it has been conspicuously successful. This is largely a result of an incorporation system pioneered there by the great Maori leader Sir Apirana Ngata. The results of his blueprint for Maori agricultural and cultural revival can be seen in prosperous small communities such as Tokomaru Bay, Ruatoria and Te Araroa.These communities also have some of the finest carved meeting houses in the country.

3

4

3. In favourable weather and with the right sea conditions, Mahia Peninsula beaches offer superb surfing. So renowned is the area for this activity that in summer surfers head there in large numbers away from other favoured beaches on the west coast. The sport has spawned a sub-culture of its own which embraces clothing, hairstyles, music and magazines, all in addition to the business of surfing itself.

4. Makorori Beach north of Gisborne, and little more than an hour away from the Mahia Peninsula beaches, is another target for surfers in summer.

1

2

1. Cape Kidnappers lies at the southern extremity of Hawke's Bay. It can be reached on foot or on horseback, or by organised safari tours from Napier. In Maori legend it was known as Te Matau-a-Maui, "Maui's fishhook." This referred to the ancestor-god said to have snagged the North Island on a hook made from his grandmother's jawbone and brought it threshing to the surface. The whole island was called "the fish of Maui". The European name was given by Cook in 1769. While his men were trading with Maoris off the cape, some of the locals tried to kidnap Taiata, a Tahitian who acted as servant to his fellow countryman, and Cook's interpreter, Tupaia. Some of the crew fired at the retreating Maori canoe and in the confusion Taiata was able to dive overboard and swim to safety.

2. Cape Kidnappers itself has been likened to the tail of a great tuatara (a lizard-like creature with a serrated back). It is best known for its gannet colony, believed to be the only mainland breeding area for this bird anywhere in the world. The birds formerly nested also on the steeper slope of the point, at some danger to their eggs. But when wildlife officers terraced that section to make it safer the birds abandoned it.

3. The breeding species is the Australian gannet. Like its cousins elsewhere in the world it is a fast and graceful bird, noted for long pointed wings and an exceedingly strong beak. It glides high over the sea in search of food. When it spots surface shoals of fish it falls on them from the sky at speeds of over 145 kilometres per hour.

3

1. Crops such as maize are taking over from more traditional farming in many parts of the country, including here on the East Coast, formerly a prominent sheep-farming area. The East Coast had a special problem. A great deal of the land was in fragmented Maori ownership. This made it difficult to get all the owners together and, once together, to agree on projects for development and production. In addition much of the land was marginal and required large-scale investment to bring it into production. The third problem was that even after these difficulties were overcome and land was carrying sheep or dairy cows, increased mechanisation on larger Pakeha farms often meant that the smaller units became progressively uneconomic. These have been some of the factors persuading owners to seek alternative forms of agriculture, especially crop growing.

2. Rural Hawke's Bay is firmly committed to large-scale sheep farming, the source of the province's early wealth when much of it was in the hands of a small number of station-owning families. The largest stations were broken up as a result of government legislation at the turn of the century. But the district remains oriented to the production of wool and sheep meat.

3. Castlepoint is yet another feature of the New Zealand coast named by Captain Cook, for reasons that are readily apparent.

1

2

Its towering rocks look very like the ruins of a European fortress. It is also one of the few landmarks along the lengthy and relatively featureless Wairarapa coast, which runs from Hawke's Bay to Wellington. In early times Castlepoint was an important meeting place for the Ngati Kahungunu tribe, and an agreement made there with the Te Atiawa from the south ensured the protection of the Pakeha settlement of Wellington in its early days. The point is best known today for its lighthouse. Built in 1913, it stands 22.6 metres high and is 51.8 metres above sea level, making it one of the tallest in the country. Its light is visible for over 30 kilometres out to sea. It is valued especially by ships coming from Panama which have no other identifiable feature to fix on.

4. Castlepoint is also valued by inland Wairarapa residents as one of the few beach resorts accessible to them. Its shelter makes it possible to keep and launch boats there, although the unpredictable action of the sea on this coast has led to fatal accidents. Until the Wellington–Masterton railway opened in 1880 Castlepoint also served as a Wairarapa port. Today one of the most keenly anticipated events for holiday makers is the summer horse races along the beach. In earlier days they were carried on without bridle and saddle. Today riders are more conventionally equipped and wear protective hats.

3

4

WELLINGTON CABLE CAR

Wellington

Wellington

Wellington, capital of the nation since 1865, has more sharply contrasting moods than any other New Zealand city. It borders Cook Strait which — in the line of the Roaring Forties — experiences more turbulent wind and sea conditions than other parts of the country's coast. Wellington city often has to bear the brunt of such weather. Wind and tide can eddy round into the harbour with almost uncontrollable ferocity, causing the conditions which sank the vessel *Wahine* in 1968 and which have put a number of other boats on to rocks in the harbour. "Windy Wellington" is the catch-cry — a term of abuse from some visitors unprepared for its gales and held up by the closure of its airport, and of affection from residents who have long since come to terms with the city's vagaries. "At least," they will tell you, "it keeps the streets clean."

In spite of all this Wellington can still turn on —

2

summer and winter — days of breathtaking stillness and charm. On these occasions a mirror harbour reflects its surrounding hills and the higher ranges behind stand out from the sky with alpine sharpness. On such days and such nights locals and visitors tend to agree that the harbour is the most beautiful in the country, and possibly in the world.

The other immediately noticeable feature of the city is its steepness. But for a small area of flat land — much of it reclaimed — close to the city centre if clings to precipitous hills. And there is no way for the capital to expand but upwards. It is hemmed by a rocky corner of the North Island with water on three sides. Most Wellingtonians seem not to mind. A local poet has noted proudly that it is one of the few places in the world where one could, if one wished, drop apple cores down ships' funnels.

The fact that it is the capital has also had an indelible effect on the city's character. The downtown area is dominated by Parliament Buildings, especially by the new Executive Wing known as the Beehive. Many of the other large buildings are headquarters of government departments. Private companies that have head offices there tend to do so because of the presence of government. The city has always been conscious of the proximity of national political figures. And of course public servants make up a large proportion of the population.

Wellingtonians seem to have fewer opportunities for outdoor recreation than other city dwellers, another consequence of local geography. The parks are few and small and there is no room for new ones. There is, however, an extensive belt of trees ringing the suburban slopes, Oriental Bay with its small beach and Edwardian elegance, good swimming and boating beaches on the eastern side of the harbour, and the golden coast with its resort communities an hour's drive to the north.

1. The first and the most spectacular way to view the capital city is by riding the Kelburn cable car. This unique vehicle lifts travellers from Lambton Quay in downtown Wellington to a superb vantage point above the university and the Botanical Gardens.

2. Oriental Bay is Wellington's only city beach. Although not as large and sandy as places such as Auckland's Mission Bay, Wellingtonians are proud of it and use it in large numbers throughout the summer.

3. Kapiti Island, seen here from the Wellington coast near Waikanae, is the country's best-known bird sanctuary.

3

1 

 2

1. The Executive Wing of Parliament Buildings is known nationally as the Beehive. It houses ministerial offices and Bellamy's, the MPs' dining room and bars. The basic design was the work of the English architect Sir Basil Spence. It has become one of the major components of the Wellington skyline. Although a source of controversy before and during its construction, Wellingtonians embrace it now even with affection.

2. Another distinctive Wellington landmark is the Carillion, which one professional guide describes as the world's largest salt shaker. It towers from the slope of the city's Mt Cook, close to the National Museum and Art Gallery and above the Basin Reserve cricket grounds. It has a large range of bells which are played from a keyboard, enabling a skilled instrumentalist to coax practically any tune from it in a cascade of bell peals.

3. Red Rocks is typical of the bleak and rugged coastline outside Wellington Harbour. Rock and stone thrown up by movements in the earth's plates have taken a massive pounding from the sea to form sharp fragments, many of the once-horizontal layers squeezed into vertical positions. The seal colony here gathers each year and allows agile visitors to get a close look at creatures that are comparatively rare this far north.

 3

4. Fishing in Wellington Harbour is not what it was in earlier years. But enthusiastic youngsters and sometimes ships' crews still try their luck from the Overseas Terminal wharf. The main business area of the city looms behind. In such conditions, with Wellington looking its deceptive best, anglers can expect to catch spotties, mullet and occasionally kahawai. These last are few and far between but well worth the fight they put up when hooked.

5. The Royal Port Nicholson Yacht Club has its boat harbour adjacent to Oriental Bay. Although the city does not support anything like the amount of sailing carried on from Auckland, Wellington yachties are a none the less dedicated group. They claim, in fact, that handling the wind and sea conditions of Wellington Harbour and Cook Strait develops more enterprise and skill than would be acquired sailing in any other part of the world.

6. The harbour's major beach resorts are on the eastern bays, opposite the city. Here yachts put out at Eastbourne, a popular bush-clad suburb and major recreation area in summer. Nearby is Days Bay, where Katherine Mansfield stayed with her family as a girl, and which inspired her story *At the Bay*.

4

5

6

1

2

1. The spectacular sight of Wellington city and harbour in early morning light from the top of Mt Victoria. This favourite spot for visitors and courting couples offers a splendid panorama of the city's unique harbour. The commercial area is spread to the left and centre. The Government centre — including Parliament Buildings, the High Court and most government department head offices — is at mid-right. This view provides a fine vista of glittering lights and reflections at night. The city itself has little nightlife by world standards, and most residents seem to want to keep it that way. When a mayor suggested the capital could benefit from a red-light district he was howled down by an outraged citizenry. This does not necessarily endear the capital to tourists. Most action at night takes place in hotel bars, of which there are a large number, many of them supporting bands. The restaurant scene has improved enormously and cuisine from most parts of the world is now available in both expensive and medium-priced eating houses. The city also promotes an especially lively theatre scene, with two professional companies and several amateur ones offering a continuous and varied range of entertainment.

2. Although Wellington is bereft of parks by comparison with other New Zealand cities, it supports a fine zoo which displays animals and birds from all over the world as well as local fauna.
Here a peacock, proverbially vain, fluffs up his tail feathers in response to admirers' attention.

The South Island

The South Island

In some respects the South Island is so unlike the North that it could be considered a different country. At each extremity it has fiords or sounds made up of high mountains and deep valleys long since inundated by a rising sea. In these aspects the island is more like Scandanavia than a South Pacific region. And there is the great backbone of the Kaikoura Range and the Southern Alps dissecting the land diagonally from north-east to south-west. This feature is not only distinctive in itself; it is responsible for the formation of the glacial valleys to the north and west, the narrow-fingered lakes in the centre of the island and the great alluvial plains to the east.

Even the Maoris have separate origin myths for the south. The North Island was said to have been fished out of the sea by Maui, the mischievous ancestor-god shared by most of Polynesia. The

South Island, however, was believed to be the canoe of Aorangi, son of the Earth Mother and Sky Father. Displeased with their parents' union, Aorangi and his brothers sailed away from Hawaiki, the traditional Polynesian homeland. In the vicinity of the South Island however, their canoe struck a reef and was wrecked. Aorangi and his brothers climbed to the higher side so as not to drown. There, waiting fruitlessly over aeons of time to be rescued by their parents, the siblings turned to stone and became the great peaks of the Alps.

The most common Maori name for the island was Te Wai Pounamu, "greenstone water". It refers to what was in Maori eyes the most precious resource there, a form of nephrite or jade. This stone was prized by Maoris for its fine cutting edge on carving tools and for its highly ornamental quality when worked into items of personal adornment, especially pendants and tiki. The stone was traded from one end of the country to the other.

The top of the island, around Golden Bay, is not unlike landscape further north. It is warm and climatically stable, and many of the limestone formations are reminiscent of those in the King Country in central North Island. The arm of Farewell Spit protects the bay and forms one of the best wading-bird sanctuaries in the country. Tasman Bay too has hot and settled weather, and its beaches have a golden sand that astonishes visitors. "Sunny Nelson" is the provincial centre and it has been able to retain many of its early buildings and much of its charm. The Marlborough Sounds to the east add a range of scenery and maritime opportunities that make the north of the South Island a source of limitless recreational pleasure.

1. Cape Farewell at the top of the South Island was named by Cook as he abandoned New Zealand in 1770 to head for Australia. Close by is the Farewell Spit bird sanctuary, a huge accumulation of sand ground down by West Coast breakers and washed northwards.

2. Kaiteriteri Beach is one of the gems of Tasman Bay. Well sheltered, it has a rich yellow sand unequalled elsewhere in the country.

3. The Kaikoura Mountains hang like a curtain over the rugged Kaikoura coastline on the eastern side of the island.

3

1

2

3

1. Picton is the centre of the Marlborough Sounds. These sunken valleys with their tall hills and deep fiords produce astounding scenery, expecially on still days. The network of waterways was originally charted in part by Cook, who twice based himself at Ship Cove at the entrance to Queen Charlotte Sound, where a memorial to him now stands. Cook also lost 10 men at Arapawa Island in the same sound in 1773. There were no witnesses to this second major clash between Maori and Pakeha. The men went to gather greens and their cannibalised remains were found the following day. Today the area offers endless opportunities for boating and fishing holidays. Its corridors are dotted with cottages, and launches bring mail and supplies to the more isolated outposts.

2. The tuatara is found on several Cook Strait Islands of the north of the South Island. Although lizard-like it is in fact a Rhynchocephalia, a surviving member of the dinosaur family. It grows to about a metre in length and is believed to live for more than 100 years. It is extinct on the mainland and strictly protected on its offshore sanctuaries.

3. The South Island pied oystercatcher flocks on beaches all over the country. Although it migrates and feeds from North

Cape to the Bluff, it breeds only in the south. Despite the name and the long bill it does not feed on oysters.

4. The beauty of Queen Charlotte Sound is especially apparent framed by trees. The bush was luxuriant in Cook's time and his botanist Joseph Banks wrote that the chorus of bellbirds was almost deafening. Today most of the bush has gone — some of it cleared for pastureland, some of it simply cleared and the land abandoned. Increasingly, however, secondary growth is regenerating, and large sections of the sound's hills are being restored to their former glory.

5. Inland from Golden Bay the Heaphy Track meanders through some of the best virgin bush in the country. Named after the pioneering surveyor Charles Heaphy, who traversed part of the district in 1846, the track begins in the rolling Gouland Downs, moves into heavy forest (part of the Northwest Nelson State Forest Park), follows the bed of the Heaphy River to the coast, and finally bursts out of the trees into a magnificent sweep of sandy coastline. It is highly regarded as one of the country's most spectacular walks.

6. The Wairau Valley, inland from the provincial town of Blenheim, has been carved out by the Wairau River. It is the flattest and most fertile district in the north of the island, and is the source of Blenheim's agricultural prosperity. At the mouth of the valley, where the river wanders into a lagoon and then out to the sea, is one of the country's most important prehistoric sites. The Wairau Bar has enabled archaeologists to build up a detailed picture of the life of the earliest Maoris, the Moa Hunters.

4

5

6

1

1. The Golden Bay coastline on the edge of Abel Tasman National Park typifies the qualities that led the Government to set aside the park in perpetuity in 1942. Rocky headlands alternate with sandy coves, and clear water lies off both. The park is a magnet in summer for visitors who want to walk the coastal track or explore the bush behind. Within an area of 22,000 hectares the park offers variety that ranges from mountainous country to lowland bush to offshore islands. It was established to commemorate the 300th anniversary of Tasman's anchorage in Golden Bay.

2. The Buller River, which runs strongly to the West Coast of the South Island, has its headwaters high among the hills of the Nelson Lakes National Park.

3. Nelson's cathedral in the centre of the provincial city has one of the most original towers in the country. The building was unusually long in construction. The foundation stone was laid by Governor-General Sir Charles Fergusson in 1925. But the church itself was not dedicated until his son Sir Bernard Fergusson was Governor-General in 1967. The initial material was Takaka marble, but rising costs and fears generated by the Murchison earthquake in 1929 led to modifications. The planned gothic tower was never built, and the final

2

3

construction material was concrete with a marble veneer. The nearby war memorial — like those in most New Zealand cities — was erected in the wake of World War I, but is used to commemorate New Zealand's participation in all wars.

4. The Maitai Valley is typical of the terrain east of Nelson. Close by is Maungatapu Mountain, scene of one of the country's most notorious slayings. Five men bringing gold dust into Nelson were killed there by the Kelly gang in 1866.

5. Shags — known as cormorants in other parts of the world — are prolific on the New Zealand coast and rivers. This one is at Collingwood in Golden Bay.

6. Lake Rotoiti is the focal point of the Nelson Lakes National Park. The other lake there is Rotoroa. Both are surrounded by steep hills which make up the bulk of the 57,000 hectare park. Rotoiti is more popular with boat users and offers more amenities.

5

4

6

Canterbury

Canterbury

The Canterbury Plains make up the largest single area of flat land in New Zealand. Formed by the deposits of widely sweeping rivers — especially the Waimakariri, the Rakaia and the Rangitata — they provide a fertile base for agriculture. The region is the major one in the country for grain growing. It is also the home of Canterbury lamb, long regarded as the best meat New Zealand produces and exports. Originally sheep were established there for wool-growing only, but the advent of refrigerated shipments to the United Kingdom in 1882 opened up a major overseas market for New Zealand meat and turned growers interests in that direction.

The higher country to the west (the foothills of the Southern Alps) is covered largely with tussock. Early efforts by run holders to burn off native vegetation for replacement with grass created

2

massive problems of erosion which have proved difficult to repair. In this area, especially in the Mackenzie Basin, lakes excavated by glaciers are a major tourist attraction and an important source of hydro-electric energy, particularly at Ohau, Tekapo and Pukaki.

Further west along the chain of the Southern Alps stand the country's great peaks. Seventeen of them exceed 3,000 metres, with the highest, Mt Cook, reaching 3,764 metres. They provide opportunities for scenic flights, for climbing, for skiing, and they are an ever-present backdrop to the lakes and townships at their feet.

The centre of Canterbury, however, is Christchurch. Founded in 1850 as an Anglican settlement by the Canterbury Association, Christchurch is more English-looking than other New Zealand cities: it has its square based on the Cathedral, the River Avon meanders through it with flower- and tree-lined banks, it has spacious parks, and it is well known for the beauty of its private gardens. In fairness it should be said that Christchurch also has industrial and manufacturing areas which produce carpets, machinery, textiles, leather goods, fertilisers, clothing and footwear. It is not all pretty and nostalgic in its aspects and prospects.

To the east of the city, over the Port Hills, lies Banks Peninsula, scenically stunning and sparsely populated. A system of ancient volcanoes, the peninsula is characterised by high hills, deep valleys and narrow inlets around the coast. The port of Lyttelton is the major settlement; others include Akaroa, Governors Bay, Diamond Harbour, Port Levy and the Maori pa of Rapaki.

Major towns to the south are Ashburton, Timaru and Waimate. Inland from these the most visible network of roads in the country intersects the plain, crosses its rivers and provides the means by which grain, meat, wool and vegetables can be carried out to markets in other parts of the country and abroad. Oddly for an area so swept by water, low rainfall and porous soil require much of the interior farmland to be extensively irrigated.

1. Christchurch, the flattest city in New Zealand, lies spread on the Canterbury Plains. The plains were laid down by soils swept off the Southern Alps and spread by a series of fanning rivers.

2. The River Avon, seen here flowing through the Christchurch Botanical Gardens, is responsible for much of the city's English appearance.

3. Christchurch's port of Lyttelton Harbour is set in an ancient volcanic crater on Banks Peninsula. It is linked to the city by the Lyttelton tunnel under the Port Hills.

3

1. Sumner Beach lies on the southern arm of the estuary formed by the Avon and Heathcote Rivers. It was originally planned as a resort for the citizens of Christchurch, which does not have a beach frontage. Sumner today is mainly of interest for its volcanic rocks and caves, especially the famous Cave Rock formed by the action of sea on ancient lava. In Maori legend the rock is identified as a petrified whale or as a taniwha. It is topped by a flagstaff that was used in earlier days to signal the state of the estuary to incoming ships. At nearby Redcliffes, Sir Julius von Haast in 1872 excavated the floor of one of the country's earliest cave shelters which led to important discoveries about the nature of Maori settlement.

2. Christchurch is blessed with one of the largest and most beautiful city parks in New Zealand. Hagley Park provides residents with a haven of peace only minutes from the city's centre. It has tree-lined walks, tow paths, tracks for joggers and horses, playing fields, a golf course, the Botanical Gardens and the Millwood Reserve, an area of shrubs and flower beds known especially for its rhododendrons and azaleas.

3. Akaroa Harbour is one of several deep indentations in Banks Peninsula that provide excellent anchorages and shelter for settlements. It also adds a unique Gallic flavour to New Zealand's story. The village was founded in 1840 as the country's only French settlement. The colonists arrived to find that British sovereignty had just been declared. They remained there, however, although the French company who owned the settlement sold out to the New Zealand Company in 1849. The French influence remains visible in Akaroa street names and in the names of Canterbury residents descended from those original colonists. Akaroa is also known for the extent to which it has retained its early architecture by preserving its late-Victorian cottages.

1

2

3

4

4. Small craft ride peacefully on safe Akaroa moorings. The harbour formerly contained a major settlement of the South Island's Ngai Tahu tribe, who used its waters to shelter and beach their canoes. Those same waters gave access to enemies, however. Te Rauparaha of Ngati Toa descended from the North Island in the trading ship *Elizabeth* in 1830 and captured the leading Ngai Tahu chief, Te Maiharanui. Ngati Toa canoes also reached Onawe Pa in the harbour two years later and the crews destroyed the settlement and ate many of the inhabitants.

5. The Christchurch Estuary provides a sheltered stretch of water on which most of the city's regattas and yacht races are held.

5

1

1. Lake Pearson, resting below the snow-clad Craigieburn Range, provides a glimpse of classic South Island landscape. Right along the east side of the Alps glacial action carved out the lakes, blocked them with silt and then filled them with water as the glaciers retreated. Lake Pearson, shaped in a flattened figure eight, is one of the smallest. It is named after Joseph Pearson, the first European to explore the area in the 1840s.

2. The Waiau River is one of the South Island's best trout- and salmon-fishing waters. It is pictured here close to Hanmer Springs, named after one of the district's early Pakeha settlers. When first located by Europeans in 1859, the thermal springs were set in bare tussock country. Early bathers hoisted an item of clothing up a flagpole to indicate which sex was in occupation of the pools. Later the area was developed as a spa, and judicious planting of exotic trees gave it a resort-like appearance. Queen Mary Hospital carried on hydrotherapy here until

2

3

1971, when the institution was turned over to the treatment of alcoholics.

3. Lake Tekapo is one of the South Island's scenic climaxes. It is known especially for the colour of its water, described as milky turquoise. This is caused by the suspension of rock dust ground by glaciers and carried into the lake by its feeder rivers. The surrounding countryside is largely tussock land, dotted with only occasional trees. To the west lie the foothills of the Alps. The gentle slopes around the lake make excellent ski fields and the area is now as popular with winter tourists as it is with summer ones. The lake lies in what is now known as the Mackenzie Country, called after a Scottish sheep stealer who allegedly took his illicit flocks there in the 1850s. His pursuers found the wide, golden tussock valleys that now bear the Scottish name, and it was opened up for English and subsequently Scottish settlers, most of whom raised sheep. The Mackenzie Country is beautiful in a desert-like way, the wind-scorched tussock reflecting a golden glow.

4. Further south in the Mackenzie Basin Mt Cook looms high over Lake Pukaki.

5. In winter Lake Tekapo presents a snow-bound aspect that some people have found European in its composition.

4

5

1

2

1. The first skiing in New Zealand was attempted in 1893 inside what is now the Mt Cook National Park. Today skiing is still carried on there but it is — from necessity — alpine skiing. The best run is that down the Tasman Glacier. Planes carry tourists and skiers to the head of the glacier, where the latter then have a fabulous 13-kilometre trip in front of them down to Ball Hut. The glacier, some 29 kilometres long and nine kilometres across at its widest point, is the longest in the country and the largest in the world to be located in a temperate zone. It is followed by the Murchison (17 kilometres), the Mueller (13 kilometres) and the Godley (also 13 kilometres). Altogether there are some 360 glaciers in the Alps, a higher number than in the European Alps.

2. Several of the South Island's major tourist hotels were deliberately sited near glaciers. Best known is the Hermitage, built near the Mueller Glacier in 1884. The original structure was destroyed by flood in 1913 and its successor by fire in 1957. The present building is one of the finest hotels in the country and attracts thousands of visitors every year. The introduction of alpine flights from the hotel over the Mt Cook National Park has given a new dimension to the area's appeal.

3

3. This mountain buttercup is one of dozens of rare alpine plants to be seen within the borders of the Mt Cook National Park. So varied is the vegetation that many botanists come to the park in spring and summer simply to walk the slopes in search of flora.

4. Mt Cook, at 3,764 metres, is the highest peak in New Zealand. Although its Maori name Aorangi has often been translated as "cloud piercer", South Island Maoris more commonly attribute it to the name of the ancestor-god reputed to have discovered the region by canoe. The mountain was called after the great navigator James Cook but not by Cook himself. The name was bestowed by Captain J. L. Stokes who completed the first survey of the New Zealand coast in the early 1850s. The first serious attempt to scale the mountain was made in 1882 by Swiss climbers who got to within 60 metres of the summit. The first successful attempt was made on Christmas Day 1894 by three New Zealand climbers, spurred on by the news that an English mountaineer with a Swiss guide was coming to the country specifically to attempt the climb. Even with the passage of years and the growth of mountaineering experience in New Zealand it remains one of the country's most challenging climbs.

4

1

2

3

1. An enthusiast on the Tasman Glacier skis down to Ball Hut after being dropped higher up the slope by plane. In general South Island skiing is better than that available in the north, and attracts more visitors from Australia and elsewhere overseas. In addition to the Tasman other favourite locations are Coronet Peak, Mt Hutt, Craigieburn Valley, Tekapo, Mt Cheeseman, Porter Heights, Erewhon and Awakino. Of these Coronet Peak has the most advanced facilities.

2. Lake Ohau on the border of Canterbury and Otago is another popular South Island ski resort. The surrounding hills fall gently towards the lake and provide ideal slopes for beginners. The Lake Ohau Lodge hotel serves as a base for the sport in winter, while in summer it acts as a fishing lodge (the lake is also well stocked with trout). Above the lake and to the north stands the Ben Ohau Range, revealing a poetic blend of Maori and Scottish traditions. In Maori legend the lake itself was formed by the weeping of two brothers whose sister had drowned at the mouth of the Waitaki River. Their tears created the lake, which in turn led to the formation of the Waitaki as its waters flowed out towards the sea.

3. Mt Sefton is another peak that is popular with climbers inside the Mt Cook National Park. It was first conquered in 1895, the year after Mt Cook was scaled. Since the 1890s the area has been used extensively by New Zealand and Australian climbers, frequently at a high cost in loss of life. It has also served as a training ground for climbers who went on to make their mark elsewhere in the world: most notably for Sir Edmund Hillary, the New Zealander who in 1953 became one of the first two men to climb Mt Everest in the Himalayas, and for New Zealanders who have taken part in Antarctic expeditions.

The West Coast

The West Coast

The West Coast of the South Island is almost a country within a country. Although much of it — especially the old province of Westland — is on the same latitude as Canterbury, and although it shares a view of the same alps, it could not contrast more sharply than it does with the South Island's eastern seaboard.

There is the terrain, for example. Where the Canterbury Plains are flat and cultivated, the West Coast is hilly and rugged. Where the plains are wide, the lowlands in the west are narrow and always close to the sea. Where the east has ports, the west has none except river mouths, of which only Greymouth is navigable — and even it is often closed by inclement weather. Where the east coast is remote from bush and mountains, the west has both in close proximity, with the slopes of the Alps falling sharply westwards to the sea. It is this close

relationship of forest and mountains, and forest and glaciers, that gives the West Coast some of its most spectacular scenery, and acts as a magnet for visitors. The best-known glaciers — Fox and Franz Josef — are in retreat, but they still extend close both to the coastal road and to the hotels built to capitalise on their beauty.

Much of the Coast is cloaked in dense forest, especially kahikatea and beech. Strong lobbying by conservationists has resulted in a great deal of it being preserved in perpetuity as part of the country's National Parks system. One area, Okarito Lagoon, is the sole breeding place for New Zealand's rare white heron and the even rarer royal spoonbill. Little lakes such as Brunner, Kaniere, Ianthe and Mapourika make up a chain of scenic gems.

Although the population on the Coast is low now, it was a boom area in the middle of the nineteenth century. The discovery of gold there in 1864 brought miners in their thousands from older fields in Otago, Coromandel and Victoria. It also attracted large numbers of Irish immigrants, another point of contrast with the more anglicised province to the east. As the gold ran out other industries were established around coal and timber and these preserved a measure of prosperity for a time. But as these extractive activities exhausted the most accessible resources by the early twentieth century, the level of prosperity and the population declined sharply.

The West Coast today presents a face of dereliction and of nature reasserting itself. The communities that remain are small but strong, independent, loyal to the Coast and hospitable in a manner that has become proverbial for its generosity. Increasingly, the area is sought out by visitors from other parts of the country and from abroad who want to experience an alternative New Zealand to that which they find elsewhere in the country.

1. Characteristic West Coast scenery shows an alpine backdrop, bush-clad foothills, a swampy river flat and tall native pines. Here Mts Tasman and Cook can be seen from close to the Fox Glacier.

2. The stretch of shore near Punakaiki is typical of terrain on the West Coast between Westport and Greymouth — a bleak and windswept area pounded by the sea and only sparsely populated.

3. The famous Pancake Rocks at Punakaiki are made of stratified limestone worn by the action of sea and wind into weird shapes.

3

1

1. After Arthur's Pass the road from Canterbury falls steeply down through the Otira Gorge, gateway to the West Coast. The gorge is the most important link between the island's east and west settlements. It includes the portal of the tunnel which carries the railway connection under the mountains. The gorge has long been a favourite with photographers and landscape artists attracted by the spectacular scenery afforded by deep folds in the foothills of the Alps and a large variety of sub-alpine vegetation.

2. Harihari, 19 kilometres south of Hokitika, is a typical West Coast farming community. It lies in a flat

2

3

4

5

river valley surrounded by steep bush-covered slopes, and it supports a timber mill. It was close to this spot that the first solo aerial crossing of the Tasman ended in 1931. Guy Lambton Menzies of Sydney flew his single-engined Avro Avian for 11 hours and 45 minutes to finish his journey upside down but safe in a swamp near Harihari. Once he was recognised the settlement gave him a hero's welcome.

3. Greymouth on the Grey River provides one of the few safe anchorages in Westland. The town became the major port for the Coast in the nineteenth century and was especially important for the shipping out of coal. The river bar, however, remains unpredictable and dangerous.

4. Weka or woodhens, rare in or absent from other areas of the country, thrive in parts of the Coast. These confident and inquisitive birds often go to great lengths to explore and search for food. They will enter huts and tents and stick their heads into cupboards and rucksacks. Their victims regard them with exasperated affection.

5. Lake Brunner is one of the most attractive of Westland's chain of little lakes. Surrounded by bush it provides a pleasant venue for swimming, boating and trout fishing.

1. The bush track around the perimeter of Lake Matheson is one of the easiest and most enjoyable walks on the West Coast. The lake was formed by a large slab of ice left behind by the retreating Fox Glacier some 14,000 years ago. The ice was insulated from the ground by a layer of gravel, and hence took a long time to melt. As it did so it slowly collapsed the gravel and sunk a massive depression into the earth. When it filled with water the depression became the lake.

2. Kaniere is another of Westland's small lakes. It too is popular in summer with swimmers, boat owners and picnickers. Water skiing and trout fishing are additional attractions. At the nearby town of Kaniere visitors can view huge tailings left behind by one of the last gold dredges to work on the Coast. More than 4,900 kilograms of the ore were extracted from the area.

3. Typical West Coast rain forest shows lush tree growth and a profusion of mosses and lichens. It takes an exceptionally high annual rainfall to sustain growth of this kind.

1

2

1

2

1. Mt Tasman and Mt Cook seen from the western side of the Alps. To the left the Fox Glacier drops towards the coast. The Alps fall away far more sharply here, giving rise to some unexpected and beautiful juxtapositions of mountains, bush and coastline.

2. Lake Matheson on an early spring morning provides its famous reflections of Mt Tasman and Mt Cook. With its fringe of bush, this West Coast scene is now a classic one.

3. The Fox Glacier cascades down the slopes of the Alps to end only a few kilometres from the coastal highway. Although like other South Island glaciers it is in retreat, there is still more than enough of it to surprise and delight visitors to the Coast.

3

Dunedin

Dunedin

More than any other city in New Zealand Dunedin has preserved its Victorian features by retaining many of its early houses and civic buildings. This gives it a distinctive character and a decided charm, and is a source of loyalty from residents and delight for visitors. Of the buildings perhaps the university is the most spectacular. It was the first to be set up in the country, in 1869. The slate roofs and bluestone walls are reminiscent of long-established British universities and date from 1879.

The city was founded at the head of Port Chalmers, which was itself an important settlement for South Island Maoris. By the late eighteenth century the Ngati Mamoe and Ngai Tahu tribes were fighting regularly in the area as the latter sought to establish pre-eminence. Violence became interracial as sealers called at the harbour and in many

instances treated the Maori inhabitants abominably. In return the Maoris took revenge, and not necessarily on the Europeans who had initially attacked them. Even today the Otago Peninsula (rendered Otakou in Maori) is a major headquarters for the Ngai Tahu people and one of their best-known pa stands near the head of the point.

The European chapter of Dunedin's history began in earnest with the formation of the Otago Association in Scotland in the 1840s and the establishment of "New Edinburgh" on the site of present-day Dunedin in 1846. The bulk of the first settlers were Scottish, many of them members of the Free Church. Their leaders were Captain William Cargill (after whom Cargill Hill overlooking the city from the north is named) and the Rev. Thomas Burns, a nephew of poet Robert Burns. Although English and Irish immigrants eventually put the Presbyterians in a minority, the Scottish character of the city largely persisted. Most of the influential city fathers were for the remainder of the nineteenth century those of Scottish origin, and they controlled the city's banking and engineering activities. Even today the Scottish antecedents are apparent in street names, in the southern dialect "r" sound, and in such city monuments as those to William Cargill and Robert Burns.

The Otago gold rush in the 1860s brought the city a burst of prosperity. Money from the fields at Gabriel's Gully, Dunstan, the Shotover and the Arrow River all passed through Dunedin, adding to its wealth and enabling the construction of many of its finest buildings and houses. Commercial activity has declined in the city in the twentieth century, however, as investment money has moved north. Dunedin today is a viable but not an expanding community. Much of its appeal for visitors comes from its architecture, its cultural institutions such as the museum and the Hocken Library, and its scenic points around the harbour, especially the albatross colony at Taiaroa Head.

1. Otago Harbour seen from the heights of the Otago Peninsula. The peninsula's length and the size of its hills provide the best anchorage in the southern part of the South Island, and were the major factor in the choice of a site for Dunedin in the 1840s.

2. Woodhaugh Gardens is one of Dunedin's parks that preserves a peaceful and rural atmosphere close to the city's streets.

3. Larnach's Castle was begun in 1871, the work of local Member of Parliament William Larnach, who became Colonial Treasurer, Minister of Public Works and Minister of Mines.

3

1

1. Moeraki on the coast north of Dunedin was the site of an important shore whaling station in the 1830s. It also became a Maori settlement as Ngai Tahu people routed by the Ngati Toa raids from the north abandoned their old homes and formed a new community. Many of them intermarried with Europeans at the station, thus forming some of the best-known South Island Maori families. On the beach close to Moeraki Point lie many of the famous Moeraki Boulders — huge spherical rocks as much as four metres in circumference and weighing several tonnes. There have been many explanations for the phenomenon. One researcher from overseas has claimed they are evidence of a visit to earth by extra-terrestial beings. Maoris identified them as petrified food baskets from one of the ancestral canoes that brought them to New Zealand from Hawaiki, the Polynesian homeland. In fact they were formed on the seabed some 60 million years ago by the accumulation of lime salts around a small centre. They fall from an eroding bank behind the beach as the softer coastal mudstone weathers away.

2. Dunedin's Scottish heritage is most dramatically apparent in the statue of Robert Burns that dominates the city's Octagon. One of the co-founders of the community was a nephew of the poet, and annual Burns' Suppers are held there still. Behind the statue stands St Paul's Anglican Cathedral, another landmark, built from Oamaru stone at the turn of the century.

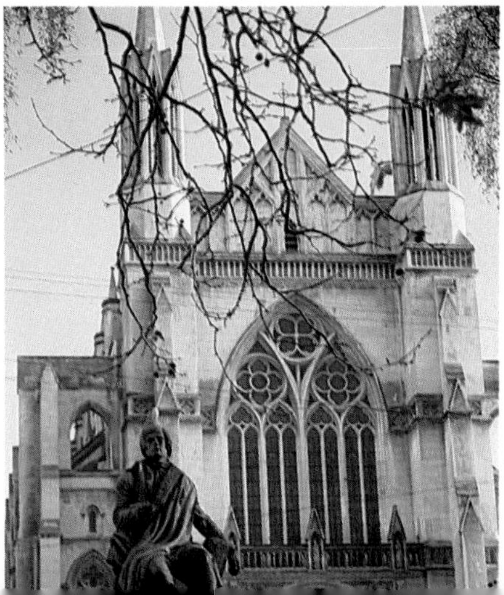

2

The South

The South

The south of the South Island has several features that have been developed more fully than in the country as a whole. One is tourism. Based on the extraordinary juxtaposition of lakes and alpine scenery, the south attracts an increasing number of visitors each year. Queenstown on Lake Wakatipu is the major centre, but the other lakes — Te Anau, Manapouri and Wanaka — all draw their share. Ski resorts, expecially Coronet Peak, add to the appeal. And in summer trout fishing, boating and swimming in the lakes are further assets. Fiordland to the west would also be an additional drawcard if its sounds were more accessible. As it is, most visitors there head for Milford Sound, which has one of the best hotels in the country. They travel by road, by air or on foot via the fabulous Milford Track. Breathtakingly beautiful Dusky and Doubtful Sounds are more difficult to reach.

The lakes and rivers of the south have made the region a vital one for the generation of hydro-electricity. This water power comes from many of the southern lakes, and from the massive Clutha and Waitaki Rivers. Round the coast fishing and crayfishing constitute a major industry, while the Bluff oysters of Foveaux Strait are world-famous for their delicacy of texture and taste.

Inland, the valleys of Central Otago have developed as a major fruit-growing region and are known especially for their peaches and apricots. Agricultural development in Southland was difficult at first because of large areas of swamp which needed draining before land could be brought into production. But intelligent development programmes were devised and the area now carries an increasing number of sheep and cattle with each successive year.

The region suffered from its first boom – caused by the Otago gold rushes — in the sense that it was too narrowly based to provide broad development. Once the gold had gone it was a long time before alternative sources of income took its place. Slowly, however, the south has established an equilibrium through a combination of agriculture, fishing, tourism and some manufacturing industries in Dunedin and Invercargill. The aluminium smelter at Bluff, which uses cheap local power to process Australian bauxite, has also made a major contribution.

To the far south, across Foveaux Strait, Stewart Island remains the last large undeveloped part of the country — a chance to see the New Zealand landscape as it was when it was wholly given over to birds and bush. And there is a national determination to preserve it this way.

1. The incomparable Milford Sound (presided over by its aptly named Mitre Peak). According to South Island Maori legend the gods placed viciously biting sandflies here to prevent humans becoming hypnotised by the beauty of the view. The sound can now be reached by road, by air and by foot, the last option over the well-known Milford Track.

2. Wanaka is another in the succession of South Island lakes with a mountainous backdrop. It feeds the Clutha River which, in its lower reaches, contains a greater volume of water than any other river in the country.

3. The Clutha Valley flats near Tarras, built up over centuries by deposits from the Clutha River.

3

1

2

3

1. Lake Wanaka from Glendhu Bay. The landscape around Wanaka is more smoothly planed by glacier action than that around other lakes. The effect is one of softness, certainly gentler to the eye than some of the more spectacularly rugged South Island views. In legend the lake was carved out of the earth by Te Rakaihautu, who travelled all over the South Island with a digging stick looking for wells. Other examples of his handiwork were said to be Te Anau, Manapouri, Wakatipu, Tekapo and Pukaki. The name Wanaka is an example of poor transcription by Europeans. The lake was named after an early Maori chief in the area, Oanaka. There is a township named after the lake close by.

2. The Cardrona Valley seen here from the Crown Range highway was formed by the Cardona River flowing out of Lake Wanaka. It was the scene of a major gold rush in 1862, which left ugly scars on the landscape at the time. Now much of the valley is manicured with grass, flowers and English trees.

3. Lake Hayes, close to Queenstown, is the best trout-fishing water in the district. It too has been framed and tamed by exotic trees in preference to native ones.

4

5

4. Waterfall Park near Arrowtown is named for its best-known feature.

5. Arrowtown is the best-preserved relic of gold-rush days to be found in New Zealand. Its miners' cottages and town buildings have been kept relatively intact from the 1860s. The Lakes District Centennial Museum — formerly the Arrowtown Bank of New Zealand — is the focal point with its pictures, furniture, mining tools and other paraphernalia from the town's boom days. The Arrowtown Gaol — much needed on account of the general brutality and lawlessness of goldfield behaviour — is also preserved. The rush that gave birth to Arrowtown began when gold was discovered on the banks of the Arrow River. The discovery was kept secret for some considerable time, but rumours of its existence began to spread when gold in large quantities was taken into Clyde by furtive prospectors, especially by an American named William Fox. As other people discovered him at work on the Arrow, Fox swore them to secrecy and dealt them in on the arrangement. The existence of the field was finally exposed when a group too large to be terrorised or controlled came upon Fox and his men in 1862. From that time the rush was on and Arrowtown sprang up virtually overnight.

1. The Treble Cone ski ground above Lake Wanaka offers the highly prized South Island powder snow. The North Island ski fields, which slush and ice over frequently, have nothing to compare with such conditions. Treble Cone also gives an unparalleled view of the lake and its surrounding country, which is touched with snow for a large part of the winter months.

2. With some 29,000 hectares of surface, Lake Wakatipu is the second largest lake in the South Island (after Te Anau) and the third in the country. Its major settlement is the tourist resort of Queenstown, which is viewed most spectacularly from the Bob's Peak cableway. In the background stand the Remarkables, a range of mountains that produce a stunning effect when they are dusted with snow. Queenstown was originally established as a sheep station. It mushroomed into a township during the Wakatipu gold rush of the 1860s. After the gold had been exhausted residents began a programme of planting and beautification to give the district an alternative attraction and source of income, and this has paid off handsomely. Some have called it the most beautiful town in New Zealand.

3. For years many of New Zealand's most rugged and boulder-strewn rivers were inaccessible to boat travellers. This was changed by the invention in the South Island of the Hamilton jet boat, a vessel of shallow draft able to propel itself speedily and safely into some of the remoter parts of the country. Jet-boat journeys have become a major feature of the South Island tourist industry. Here visitors ascend the Shotover Gorge not far from Queenstown. This river, the major scene of the Wakatipu gold rush, was named after a property of the same name near Oxford.

4. Coronet Peak above Queenstown is the country's best-known and most heavily patronised ski field. From the peak itself (1,619 metres) to the lower slopes its dry powder snow is prized. Further drawcards are the beauty of nearby Queenstown and the comforts and accommodation it offers. The skiing season here extends from July to September. Buses bring sports enthusiasts to the lower slopes from Queenstown and a chairlift carries them up a

1

2

3

4

further 450 metres, almost to the summit. For movement about the lower slopes there are poma lifts and ski tows. The chairlift also operates during the summer so that visitors can take advantage of the views at that time of the year too.

5. The steamer ***Earnslaw*** which carries tourists across Lake Wakatipu is all that remains of a fleet of boats that used to ply the lake in the nineteenth century. They transported passengers from Kingston at the south end to Queenstown and Glenorchy to the north. Their patronage was guaranteed because there was no road around the lake until the 1930s, and the railway went only as far as Kingston. The last-but-one survivor of the fleet was the paddlesteamer ***Mountaineer***, which operated for nearly 60 years before being withdrawn from service in 1932.

5

1

2

1. Some of the most rewarding but also the best-hidden scenery around Wakatipu can be found at the head of the lake, on the Glenorchy road. Here, approaching Glenorchy, Mt Earnslaw rears up, unusually isolated in comparison with other South Island peaks. The steamer on the lake is named after it.

2. Lighthouse Rock is one of the dominating features close to the precipitous Skippers Road. The Skippers Gorge was the scene of one of the country's most arduous gold rushes. Conditions in the steep narrow valley were at times appalling. It was reached by a dangerous bridle track, from which horses and men frequently fell. Once in the gorge miners had to struggle constantly for footholds as they panned and prospected up bleak ravines. Winter conditions were especially punishing as icy winds swept through the gorge and deposited snow. Many men perished here and were left behind in the Skippers Cemetery. For all this, many prospectors still believed the result was worth the effort and the danger. Gold was found in quantity and quality. The miners claimed that each square foot of the bed of the gorge yielded up at least an ounce of ore. Such a reputation meant that in addition to the privations supplied by nature, over-crowding was another. Chinese workers also came here in large numbers, especially to re-work parts of the bed that European prospectors had passed over quickly and not always thoroughly. The road through Skippers today is scarcely less frightening than the original bridle track. It is narrow and tortuous and hangs over enormous drops in places. It should be attempted only with patience and care.

3. The Eglinton Valley runs close to Lake Te Anau on the road to Milford Sound. Its thick bush and alpine prospects provide one of the most rewarding drives in the country.

4. This sight of the Sutherland Falls is one of the highlights for walkers

3

4

of the Milford Track. Dropping 580.3 metres in three stages, the falls are the highest in New Zealand and among the highest in the world. They are named after their discoverer Donald Sutherland, also known as the Hermit of Milford, who was the first person to live permanently at the sound.

5. Another popular resting place on the Milford Track is the Giant Gate Falls. Many of those who have completed the track declare that it is the finest walk in the world.

5

1

1. Lupins bloom on the shore of Lake Manapouri. The lake became the subject of controversy in the 1960s when the Government of the day prepared to raise it for the generation of electricity. A national outcry prevented this measure and it remains today largely unspoiled.

2. Queen's Gardens in Invercargill is the Southland capital's major park.

3. First Church in Invercargill points to the city's Scottish antecedents. It was named after the founder of Dunedin, William Cargill.

4. Dawn at Halfmoon Bay, Stewart Island, the only inhabited part of New Zealand's most southern coastline. When Cook first circumnavigated the country in 1770 he made in this region one of his few major mistakes in charting: he believed that Stewart Island was attached to the South

2

3

4

Island and rendered it so on his map. It is not known for certain when the error was discovered and rectified, nor exactly how the island received its name. Certainly by the turn of the nineteenth century sealers were calling at the island and, later, whalers too landed there. Most early exploitation of the island was for its timber, which was milled until the turn of the twentieth century. Tin and gold were also mined for a time at Port Pegasus.

5. The settlement of Oban in Halfmoon Bay is the only one on the island, its permanent population a little over 300 people. Most of them draw their living from the sea, from commercial fishing. In summer the numbers swell with an influx of South Island visitors, many of whom own cribs (holiday cottages) in the bay. The island is linked to the mainland by the ferry ***Wairua*** which crosses from Bluff several times a week. There is also an air service from Invercargill. There are no roads, apart from one around Halfmoon Bay, so travel around the island is necessarily by launch or on foot.

5

the origin of emotions

version 1.0

mark devon

the origin of emotions

version 1.0

ISBN 1-4196-4727-X

LCCN 2006901093

www.amazon.com

www.amazon.co.uk

www.booksurge.com

www.theoriginofemotions.com

TABLE OF CONTENTS

Table of Contents

Table of Contents

Chapter I

Introduction

The Origin of Emotions identifies each emotion's purpose, trigger and effect.

This is a sample of the assertions made in this book:

- mothers only love their children for 33 months
- men only love a woman for 42 months
- only women feel infatuation and heartbreak
- only men feel jealousy
- you feel revenge when a rule breaker harms you
- you stop feeling revenge when you retaliate
- you feel pride when your rank rises
- you feel humiliation when your rank falls
- you feel humor when another person's rank falls
- you feel envy when a peer's rank rises above yours
- you are always doing what is best for the species

CHAPTER 2

FIVE TYPES OF EMOTION

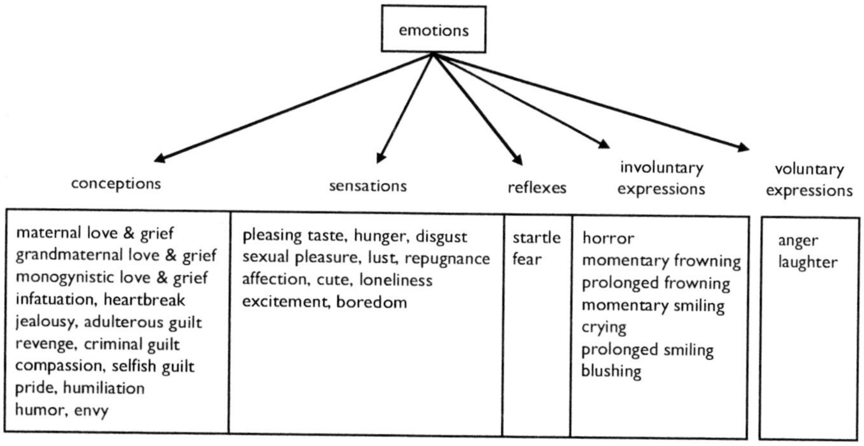

There are five types of emotion: conceptions, sensations, reflexes, involuntary expressions and voluntary expressions.

Conceptions, sensations, reflexes and involuntary expressions are biological adaptations. They are transmitted to the next generation through reproduction. They are universal to the species.

Voluntary expressions are cultural adaptations. They are transmitted to the next generation through interaction. They vary by culture.

	conceptions	sensations	reflexes	involuntary expressions	voluntary expressions
	maternal love & grief grandmaternal love & grief monogynistic love & grief infatuation, heartbreak jealousy, adulterous guilt revenge, criminal guilt compassion, selfish guilt pride, humiliation humor, envy	pleasing taste, hunger, disgust sexual pleasure, lust, repugnance affection, cute, loneliness excitement, boredom	startle fear	horror momentary frowning prolonged frowning momentary smiling crying prolonged smiling blushing	anger laughter
purpose	direct your behavior	direct your behavior	help you avoid threats	direct behavior of others	direct behavior of others
trigger	conclusions	sensory stimuli	conclusions or sensory stimuli	conception, sensation or reflex	habitual decision
mental effects	positive or negative	positive or negative	suppressive	none	none
physical effects	none	almost none	defensive	facial expressions	facial & vocal expressions

Conceptions direct your behavior.

Conceptions are positive or negative mental effects that are triggered by conclusions.

Maternal love is a positive effect triggered by the conclusion "my child is happy". Maternal grief is a negative effect triggered by the conclusion "my child is dead".

Conceptions can also be triggered by imagining a conclusion. Maternal grief can be triggered by imagining the conclusion "my child is dead".

Conceptions do not trigger physical effects. Conceptions do not need to trigger physical effects to direct your behavior.

A few conceptions do trigger involuntary expressions, which have a different purpose.

	conceptions	sensations	reflexes	involuntary expressions	voluntary expressions
	maternal love & grief grandmaternal love & grief monogynistic love & grief infatuation, heartbreak jealousy, adulterous guilt revenge, criminal guilt compassion, selfish guilt pride, humiliation humor, envy	pleasing taste, hunger, disgust sexual pleasure, lust, repugnance affection, cute, loneliness excitement, boredom	startle fear	horror momentary frowning prolonged frowning momentary smiling crying prolonged smiling blushing	anger laughter
purpose	direct your behavior	direct your behavior	help you avoid threats	direct behavior of others	direct behavior of others
trigger	conclusions	sensory stimuli	conclusions or sensory stimuli	conception, sensation or reflex	habitual decision
mental effects	positive or negative	positive or negative	suppressive	none	none
physical effects	none	almost none	defensive	facial expressions	facial & vocal expressions

Sensations direct your behavior.

Sensations are positive or negative mental effects that are triggered by the presence or absence of sensory stimuli.

Pleasing taste is a positive effect triggered by the taste of food. Hunger is a negative effect triggered by the absence of food. Disgust is a negative effect triggered by the smell of toxins, such as fecal matter.

Sensations can be triggered by stimuli that is real, recorded, remembered or imagined. Men feel sexual pleasure when they see a naked woman whether she is real, recorded, remembered or imagined.

Sensations trigger almost no physical effects. A few sensations do trigger minor physical effects, like salivation. However, sensations do not trigger any major physical effects, like increased heart rate. Sensations do not need to trigger physical effects to direct your behavior.

A few sensations do trigger involuntary expressions, which have a different purpose.

conceptions	sensations	reflexes	involuntary expressions	voluntary expressions
maternal love & grief grandmaternal love & grief monogynistic love & grief infatuation, heartbreak jealousy, adulterous guilt revenge, criminal guilt compassion, selfish guilt pride, humiliation humor, envy	pleasing taste, hunger, disgust sexual pleasure, lust, repugnance affection, cute, loneliness excitement, boredom	startle fear	horror momentary frowning prolonged frowning momentary smiling crying prolonged smiling blushing	anger laughter

purpose	direct your behavior	direct your behavior	help you avoid threats	direct behavior of others	direct behavior of others
trigger	conclusions	sensory stimuli	conclusions or sensory stimuli	conception, sensation or reflex	habitual decision
mental effects	positive or negative	positive or negative	suppressive	none	none
physical effects	none	almost none	defensive	facial expressions	facial & vocal expressions

Reflexes help you avoid threats.

Reflexes are triggered by conclusions or sensory stimuli. Fear can be triggered by the conclusion "a man is pointing a loaded gun at me". Fear can also be triggered by the sight of a snake.

Reflexes trigger a mental effect that suppresses conceptions and sensations. When you are frightened, you cannot feel sexual pleasure or humiliation. Suppression helps you concentrate on avoiding a threat by eliminating distractions.

Reflexes trigger defensive physical effects. Startle involuntarily tenses neck muscles, which prevents tearing by a predator's claws or talons. Fear releases adrenalin to increase heart rate, which helps fight or flight.

Reflexes are the only emotions that trigger major physical effects.

	conceptions	sensations	reflexes	involuntary expressions	voluntary expressions
	maternal love & grief grandmaternal love & grief monogynistic love & grief infatuation, heartbreak jealousy, adulterous guilt revenge, criminal guilt compassion, selfish guilt pride, humiliation humor, envy	pleasing taste, hunger, disgust sexual pleasure, lust, repugnance affection, cute, loneliness excitement, boredom	startle fear	horror momentary frowning prolonged frowning momentary smiling crying prolonged smiling blushing	anger laughter
purpose	direct your behavior	direct your behavior	help you avoid threats	direct behavior of others	direct behavior of others
trigger	conclusions	sensory stimuli	conclusions or sensory stimuli	conception, sensation or reflex	habitual decision
mental effects	positive or negative	positive or negative	suppressive	none	none
physical effects	none	almost none	defensive	facial expressions	facial & vocal expressions

Involuntary expressions direct the behavior of others.

Involuntary expressions are triggered by a conception, sensation or reflex. The reflex of fear triggers the involuntary expression of horror.

Involuntary expressions have a different purpose than their trigger emotion. Fear helps you avoid threats. The expression of horror on your face helps others avoid threats.

conceptions	sensations	reflexes	involuntary expressions	voluntary expressions
maternal love & grief grandmaternal love & grief monogynistic love & grief infatuation, heartbreak jealousy, adulterous guilt revenge, criminal guilt compassion, selfish guilt pride, humiliation humor, envy	pleasing taste, hunger, disgust sexual pleasure, lust, repugnance affection, cute, loneliness excitement, boredom	startle fear	horror momentary frowning prolonged frowning momentary smiling crying prolonged smiling blushing	anger laughter

	conceptions	sensations	reflexes	involuntary expressions	voluntary expressions
purpose	direct your behavior	direct your behavior	help you avoid threats	direct behavior of others	direct behavior of others
trigger	conclusions	sensory stimuli	conclusions or sensory stimuli	conception, sensation or reflex	habitual decision
mental effects	positive or negative	positive or negative	suppressive	none	none
physical effects	none	almost none	defensive	facial expressions	facial & vocal expressions

Voluntary expressions direct the behavior of others.

Voluntary expressions are triggered by habitual decision. Anger is a habitual response to feeling revenge. Laughter is a habitual response to feeling humor. These expressions seem involuntary because they are deeply ingrained habits, like walking or talking.

Voluntary expressions are better than speech. Anger is more credible than calmly stating "I am being coerced by revenge to harm you". Laughter can be understood more easily than an audience of people simultaneously saying "I feel humor".

CHAPTER 3

THREE CATEGORIES OF PURPOSE

emotions

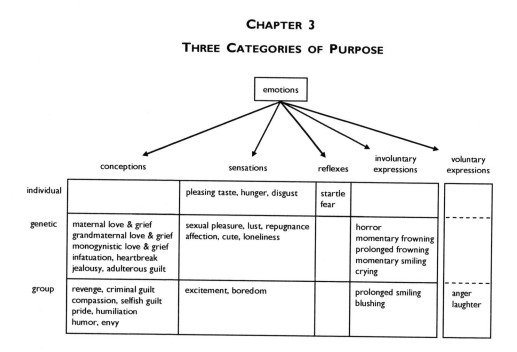

	conceptions	sensations	reflexes	involuntary expressions	voluntary expressions
individual		pleasing taste, hunger, disgust	startle fear		
genetic	maternal love & grief grandmaternal love & grief monogynistic love & grief infatuation, heartbreak jealousy, adulterous guilt	sexual pleasure, lust, repugnance affection, cute, loneliness		horror momentary frowning prolonged frowning momentary smiling crying	
group	revenge, criminal guilt compassion, selfish guilt pride, humiliation humor, envy	excitement, boredom		prolonged smiling blushing	anger laughter

Emotions fall into three categories of purpose: individual, genetic and group.

	conceptions	sensations	reflexes	involuntary expressions	voluntary expressions
individual		pleasing taste, hunger, disgust	startle fear		
genetic	maternal love & grief grandmaternal love & grief monogynistic love & grief infatuation, heartbreak jealousy, adulterous guilt	sexual pleasure, lust, repugnance affection, cute, loneliness		horror momentary frowning prolonged frowning momentary smiling crying	
group	revenge, criminal guilt compassion, selfish guilt pride, humiliation humor, envy	excitement, boredom		prolonged smiling blushing	anger laughter

Individual emotions help you.

Individual emotions encourage eating and avoiding physical harm.

Individual sensations encourage you to eat and avoid toxins. Pleasing taste and hunger encourage eating. Disgust encourages avoiding toxins.

Reflexes help you avoid threats. Startle mitigates the harm of a predator's initial strike. Fear helps fight or flight.

Eating and avoiding physical harm are the only behaviors that help your survival. All other behaviors harm your survival to help your genes or your group.

	conceptions	sensations	reflexes	involuntary expressions	voluntary expressions
individual		pleasing taste, hunger, disgust	startle fear		
genetic	maternal love & grief grandmaternal love & grief monogynistic love & grief infatuation, heartbreak jealousy, adulterous guilt	sexual pleasure, lust, repugnance affection, cute, loneliness		horror momentary frowning prolonged frowning momentary smiling crying	
group	revenge, criminal guilt compassion, selfish guilt pride, humiliation humor, envy	excitement, boredom		prolonged smiling blushing	anger laughter

Genetic emotions help your genes.

Genetic conceptions encourage post-natal care. Maternal love and grief encourage the feeding and protection of children. Grandmaternal love and grief encourage the feeding and protection of grandchildren. Monogynistic love and grief encourage the support and protection of mothers. Infatuation and heartbreak encourage the activation of monogynistic love. Jealousy and adulterous guilt encourage the punishment or avoidance of maternal infidelity.

Genetic sensations encourage mating and kin interaction. Sexual pleasure, lust and repugnance encourage mating with non-kin. Affection, cute and loneliness encourage interaction with kin.

Genetic involuntary expressions warn kin or encourage kin interaction. Horror and momentary frowning warn kin about threats. Prolonged frowning warns kin about grief by making it tangible. Momentary smiling and crying encourage kin interaction.

	conceptions	sensations	reflexes	involuntary expressions	voluntary expressions
individual		pleasing taste, hunger, disgust	startle fear		
genetic	maternal love & grief grandmaternal love & grief monogynistic love & grief infatuation, heartbreak jealousy, adulterous guilt	sexual pleasure, lust, repugnance affection, cute, loneliness		horror momentary frowning prolonged frowning momentary smiling crying	
group	revenge, criminal guilt compassion, selfish guilt pride, humiliation humor, envy	excitement, boredom		prolonged smiling blushing	anger laughter

Group emotions help your group.

Groups are non-kin you cooperate with. Groups include communities, religions, countries, companies, professions, colleges and social clubs.

Group conceptions encourage maximizing group efficiency. Revenge and criminal guilt encourage the punishment or avoidance of rule breaking. Compassion and selfish guilt encourage helping the unfortunate, which reduces insurance costs. Pride, humiliation, humor and envy encourage maximizing rank, which measures your expected contribution to group happiness.

Group sensations encourage maximizing group territory. Excitement and boredom encourage exploring for new scenery.

Group involuntary expressions encourage maximizing rank. Prolonged smiling makes pride tangible to others. Blushing mitigates humiliation during trial-and-error.

Voluntary expressions usually follow a group emotion. Anger usually follows revenge. Laughter usually follows humor.

Chapter 4

Conceptions

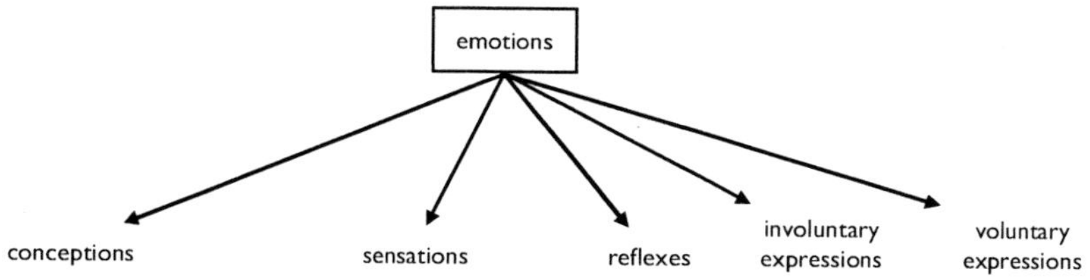

	conceptions	sensations	reflexes	involuntary expressions	voluntary expressions
individual		pleasing taste, hunger, disgust	startle fear		
genetic	maternal love & grief grandmaternal love & grief monogynistic love & grief infatuation, heartbreak jealousy, adulterous guilt	sexual pleasure, lust, repugnance affection, cute, loneliness		horror momentary frowning prolonged frowning momentary smiling crying	
group	revenge, criminal guilt compassion, selfish guilt pride, humiliation humor, envy	excitement, boredom		prolonged smiling blushing	anger laughter

	conceptions	sensations	reflexes	involuntary expressions	voluntary expressions
purpose	direct your behavior	direct your behavior	help you avoid threats	direct behavior of others	direct behavior of others
trigger	conclusions	sensory stimuli	conclusions or sensory stimuli	conception, sensation or reflex	habitual decision
mental effects	positive or negative	positive or negative	suppressive	none	none
physical effects	none	almost none	defensive	facial expressions	facial & vocal expressions

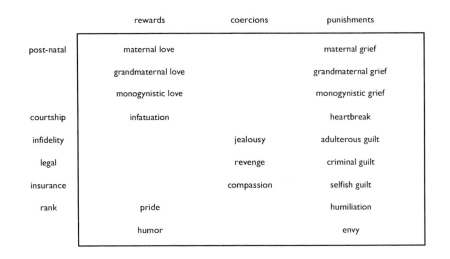

	rewards	coercions	punishments
post-natal	maternal love		maternal grief
	grandmaternal love		grandmaternal grief
	monogynistic love		monogynistic grief
courtship	infatuation		heartbreak
infidelity		jealousy	adulterous guilt
legal		revenge	criminal guilt
insurance		compassion	selfish guilt
rank	pride		humiliation
	humor		envy

There are three types of conception: rewards, coercions and punishments.

Rewards are positive effects triggered by a conclusion. Maternal love is a positive effect triggered by the conclusion "my child is happy".

Coercions are negative effects triggered by one conclusion and stopped by another. Revenge is a negative effect triggered by the conclusion "X harmed me by breaking the rules". Revenge is stopped by the conclusion "I harmed X as much as X harmed me".

Punishments are negative effects triggered by a conclusion. Maternal grief is a negative effect triggered by the conclusion "my child is dead".

Conceptions begin to be triggered at month 24, when conceptual thought is possible. At this age, children begin to feel the group conceptions: revenge, criminal guilt, compassion, selfish guilt, pride, humiliation, humor and envy. The onset of conceptions is the first of four reasons for the terrible-two's. The other reasons are: the end of maternal love, the end of cute and the onset of conceptual fear.

Conceptions fall into six categories of purpose: post-natal, courtship, infidelity, legal, insurance and rank.

	rewards	coercions	punishments
post-natal	maternal love		maternal grief
	grandmaternal love		grandmaternal grief
	monogynistic love		monogynistic grief

Post-natal conceptions encourage the feeding and protection of children and mothers. Maternal love rewards mothers for feeding children. Maternal grief punishes mothers if children die. Grandmaternal love rewards grandmothers for helping with the feeding of grandchildren. Grandmaternal grief punishes grandmothers if grandchildren die. Monogynistic love rewards men for supporting women. Monogynistic grief punishes men if women die.

	rewards	coercions	punishments
courtship	infatuation		heartbreak

Courtship conceptions activate monogynistic love. Infatuation rewards women for activating a man's monogynistic love. Heartbreak punishes women if they fail to activate monogynistic love.

	rewards	coercions	punishments
infidelity		jealousy	adulterous guilt

Infidelity conceptions discourage female infidelity. Jealousy coerces men to punish women for infidelity. Adulterous guilt punishes philandering women directly.

	rewards	coercions	punishments
legal		revenge	criminal guilt

Legal conceptions reduce rule breaking. Revenge coerces victims to punish rule breakers. Criminal guilt punishes rule breakers directly.

	rewards	coercions	punishments
insurance		compassion	selfish guilt

Insurance conceptions encourage helping the unfortunate. Compassion coerces you to help the unfortunate. Selfish guilt punishes you if you fail to help the unfortunate.

	rewards	coercions	punishments
rank	pride		humiliation
	humor		envy

Rank conceptions encourage maximizing rank. Pride rewards you for increasing your rank. Humiliation punishes you for not maintaining your rank. Humor rewards you for learning about rank-reducing mistakes that others make. Envy punishes you when a peer's rank rises above yours.

The rank conceptions are the main reason we compete and cooperate.

Chapter 5

Maternal Love

Type of Emotion:	conceptual reward
Conceptual Trigger:	" my child is happy "
Mental Effect:	positive
Key Features:	the happier the child, the stronger the effect has a duration of 33 months for each child

Purpose

Maternal love primarily encourages mothers to breastfeed their children. It secondarily encourages mothers to teach their children.

Conceptual Trigger

	conceptions	sensations	reflexes	involuntary expressions	voluntary expressions
individual		pleasing taste, hunger, disgust	startle fear		
genetic	maternal love & grief grandmaternal love & grief monogynistic love & grief infatuation, heartbreak jealousy, adulterous guilt	sexual pleasure, lust, repugnance affection, cute, loneliness		horror momentary frowning prolonged frowning momentary smiling crying	
group	revenge, criminal guilt compassion, selfish guilt pride, humiliation humor, envy	excitement, boredom		prolonged smiling blushing	anger laughter

Maternal love is triggered by a child's happiness. Happiness is a summary term. If someone is happy, they feel a positive effect. If someone is unhappy, they feel a negative effect.

Eating is the primary source of happiness for children under 24 months. Children do not feel conceptions until 24 months. They do not feel sexual sensations until puberty. They do not feel cute until 33 months. Consequently, the only positive or negative sensations they feel are: pleasing taste, hunger, disgust, affection, loneliness, excitement and boredom. Of these sensations, pleasing taste and hunger are usually the strongest.

Teaching is a secondary source of happiness. If a child has recently been fed, the strongest sensations it will feel are affection, loneliness, excitement and boredom. Children feel affection when they interact with their mothers and loneliness if they do not. Children feel excitement when they see new scenery and boredom if they do not.

Maternal love is triggered regardless of who makes a child happy. Maternal love is triggered by "my child is happy", not by "I made my child happy". This ensures mothers do what is best for their child. If maternal love was triggered by "I made my child happy", mothers would not feel love when grandmothers cared for their children.

Mental Effect

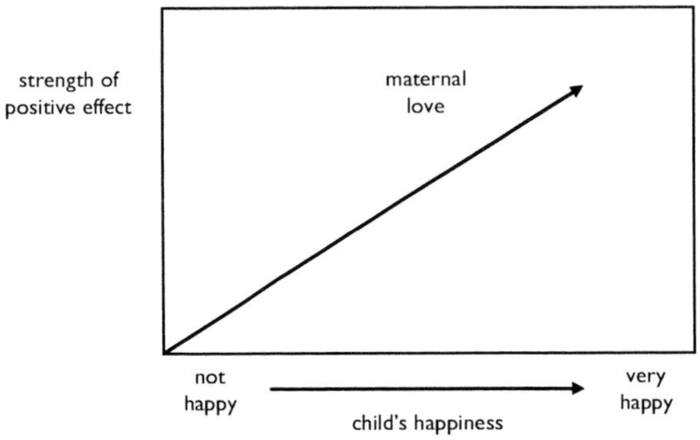

Maternal love varies with a child's happiness. The happier a child is, the stronger the positive effect. Mothers feel stronger love when they see their children smile.

Maternal love varies with a child's happiness to maximize a child's development. To maximize the love they feel, mothers do what maximizes a child's happiness. The happier a child is, the faster it will develop. The more a child enjoys food, the more nutritional it is. The more a child enjoys affection, the more intensive the interaction. The more a child enjoys excitement, the more novel the scenery.

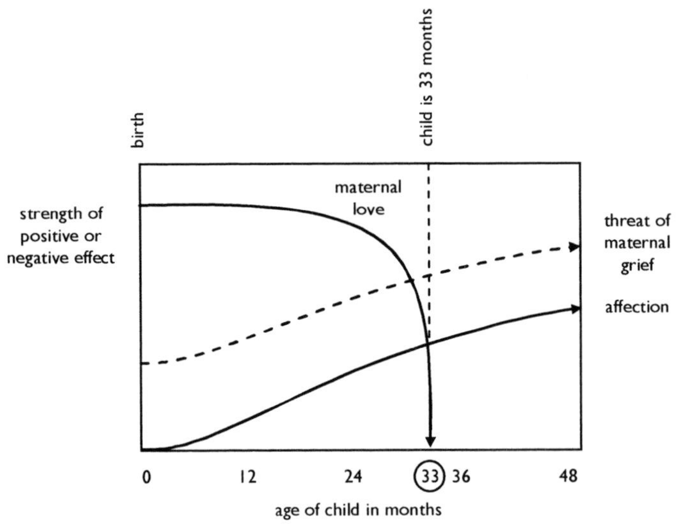

Maternal love stops when a child is 33 months old. Mothers maximize their reproduction by focusing on the next child when the current child can feed itself. By 33 months, children can feed themselves if food is available. They can walk and their first set of teeth have completed eruption.

The natural duration of breastfeeding is 33 months, as surveys of non-Western societies have shown. *A Time to Wean: The Hominid Blueprint for the Natural Age of Weaning in Modern Human Populations (Breastfeeding – Biocultural Perspectives)* by Katherine Dettwyler explores this subject indepth.

Affection continues after 33 months. Affection is the positive effect that mothers continue to feel when they see or hear their children. Affection usually grows stronger over time. However, it never reaches the strength of maternal love.

The threat of maternal grief also continues after 33 months.

The end of maternal love is the second of four reasons for the terrible-two's. When a child is 33 months old, mothers no longer receive a hit of maternal love when they make their child happy.

<u>Other Species</u>

Species feel maternal love if mothers feed their offspring. All mammals and most birds feel maternal love.

<u>Kissing</u>

Kissing is a cultural adaptation that evolved from the maternal transfer of masticated food. Before pablum, mothers chewed solid food and then transferred it to their children by putting their mouths directly on their child's mouth. The transfer was emotional for both mother and child. Both felt affection and pleasing taste. Mothers also felt maternal love. Because mouth-mating was a universal experience, it was also universally recognized as a signal of positive emotions.

CHAPTER 6

MATERNAL GRIEF

Type of Emotion:	conceptual punishment
Conceptual Trigger:	" my child is dead "
Mental Effect:	negative
Key Feature:	the closer the child was to puberty, the stronger the effect
Involuntary Expression:	prolonged frowning
Synonym:	sorrow

Purpose

Maternal grief encourages mothers to protect their children.

Maternal love and maternal grief are different.

Maternal love lasts 33 months. The threat of maternal grief lasts forever. Mothers do not nag their older children because they love them. Mothers nag them to avoid grief.

Maternal love encourages maximum effort. Maternal grief encourages minimum effort. A mother feels more maternal love if she makes her child happier. A mother does not reduce the threat of maternal grief if she makes a safe child safer. Maternal grief encourages minimum effort to maximize the number of children mothers give birth to. The more time mothers spend protecting older children, the fewer children they have.

Maternal love encourages keeping a child happy. Maternal grief encourages keeping a child alive. Mothers do not vaccinate their children to make them happy. Mothers vaccinate children to keep them alive.

Conceptual Trigger

Maternal grief is triggered by a child's death, whether the mother could have prevented it or not. This encourages mothers to treat all death as preventable. Mothers want to know if power lines cause leukemia.

Like all conceptions, maternal grief can be triggered by imagining its conceptual trigger. Mothers trigger imagined grief when they lose their child in a shopping mall. The relief they feel when they find their missing child is the end of imagined grief.

Imagined grief is more important than actual grief. Actual grief only affects the mothers of dead children. Imagined grief affects all mothers. The prolonged frowning triggered by maternal grief helps other mothers imagine grief's negative effect.

Mental Effect

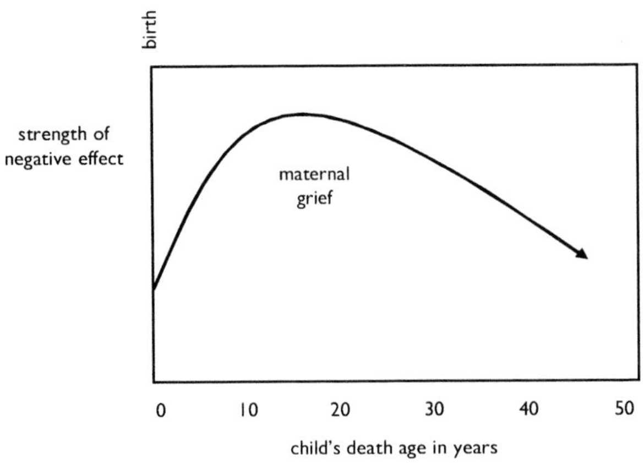

Maternal grief varies with a child's death age. The closer a child was to puberty, the stronger the negative effect. Mothers whose children die as teenagers feel the strongest grief.

Grief varies with a child's reproductive value. The closer a child is to puberty, the higher its reproductive value. A 16 year old has survived childhood and still has 100% of its reproductive capacity. *Human Grief: Is its Intensity Related to the Reproductive Value of the Deceased?* is a study led by Charles Crawford of Simon Fraser University that probed the relationship between grief and death age.

Maternal grief causes mothers to favor their first born over other children. First born children are usually the closest to puberty and therefore trigger the strongest grief if they die.

Other Species

Species feel maternal grief if mothers protect their offspring. Crocodiles feel maternal grief, but not maternal love. Crocodile mothers do not feed their young, but they do protect them by gingerly holding them in their jaws when a threat lurks.

CHAPTER 7

GRANDMATERNAL LOVE

Type of Emotion:	conceptual reward
Conceptual Trigger:	" my grandchild is happy "
Mental Effect:	positive
Key Features:	not triggered in pre-menopausal grandmothers the happier the grandchild, the stronger the effect has a duration of 33 months for each grandchild

Purpose

Grandmaternal love encourages grandmothers to help feed their grandchildren. Grandmothers primarily help by sharing experience.

Conceptual Trigger

Grandmaternal love is not triggered in pre-menopausal grandmothers. Pre-menopausal women maximize their reproduction by having more children.

Pre-menopausal grandmothers do feel cute and affection when they see grandchildren. These positive effects are mistakenly believed to be grandmaternal love.

Maternal love and grandmaternal love cause helpful conflict. Both are triggered by the happiness of the same child. This causes mothers and grandmothers to compete to make the child happy. Their competition helps maximize the child's development.

Mental Effect

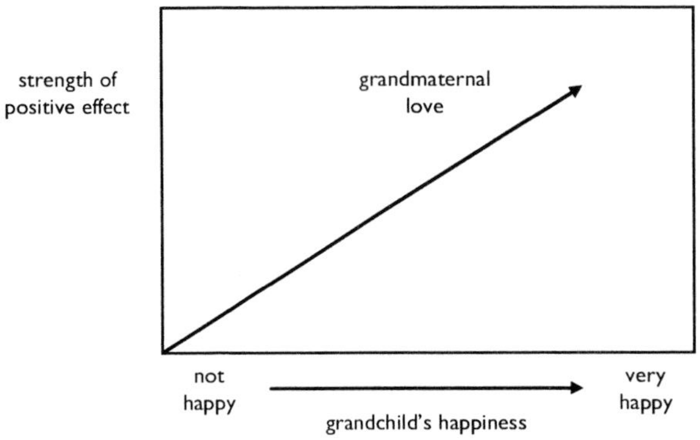

Grandmaternal love varies with a grandchild's happiness. The happier a grandchild is, the stronger the positive effect. Grandmothers feel stronger love when they see their grandchildren smile.

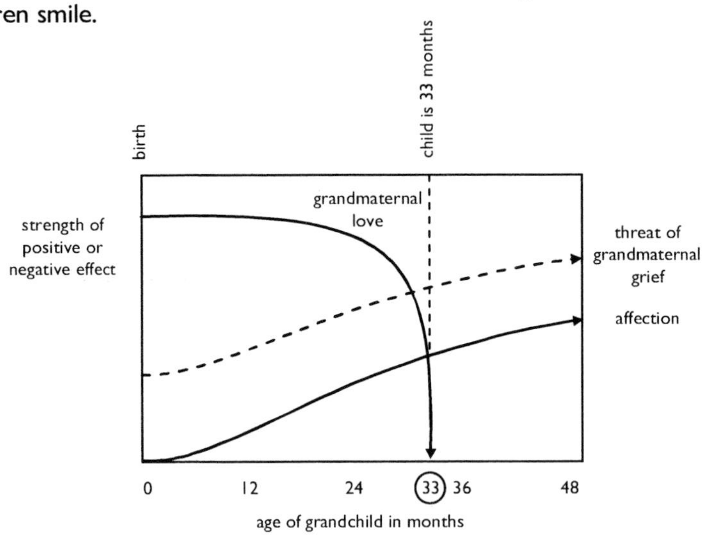

Grandmaternal love stops when a grandchild is 33 months old. Like mothers, grandmothers maximize their reproduction by focusing on the next grandchild when the current grandchild can feed itself.

Affection and the threat of grandmaternal grief continue after 33 months.

Chapter 8

Grandmaternal Grief

Type of Emotion:	conceptual punishment
Conceptual Trigger:	" my grandchild is dead "
Mental Effect:	negative
Key Features:	not triggered in pre-menopausal grandmothers the closer the child was to puberty, the stronger the effect
Involuntary Expression:	prolonged frowning
Synonym:	sorrow

<u>Purpose</u>

Grandmaternal grief encourages grandmothers to help protect their grandchildren. Grandmothers primarily help by sharing experience.

<u>Conceptual Trigger</u>

Grandmaternal grief is not triggered in pre-menopausal grandmothers. Pre-menopausal grandmothers maximize their reproduction by having more children.

Pre-menopausal grandmothers may feel loneliness when a grandchild dies. This negative effect is mistakenly believed to be grandmaternal grief.

Grandmaternal grief is triggered by a grandchild's death, whether the grandmother could have prevented it or not. This encourages grandmothers to treat all death as preventable. Grandmothers also want to know if power lines cause leukemia.

Mental Effect

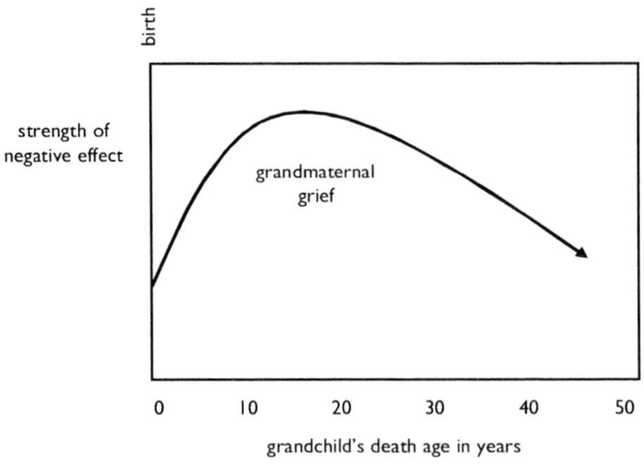

Grandmaternal grief varies with a grandchild's death age. The closer a grandchild was to puberty, the stronger the negative effect. Grandmothers whose grandchildren die as teenagers feel the strongest grief.

Other Species

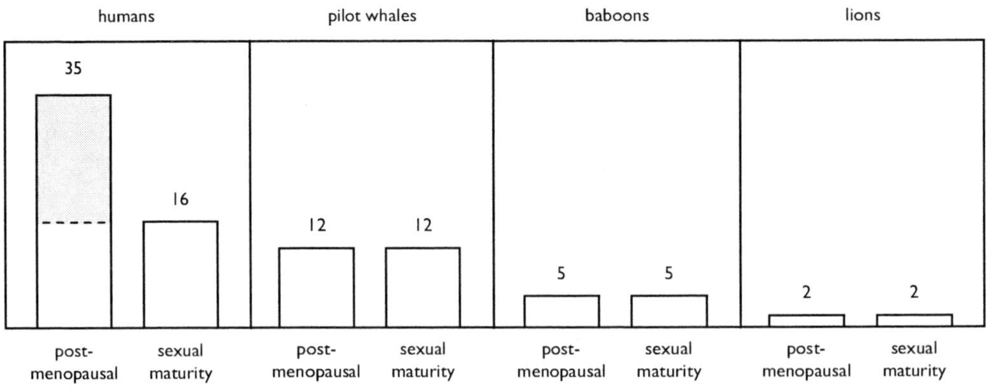

Other species do not feel grandmaternal love and grief. Grandmothers have not evolved in other species, but good mothers have.

Grandmothers are post-menopausal beyond the sexual maturity of their last born. Humans are post-menopausal for 35 years and need 16 years to reach sexual maturity.

Good mothers are only post-menopausal long enough for their last born to reach sexual maturity, but not beyond. Examples of good mothers include pilot whales, baboons and lions. Pilot whales are post-menopausal for 12 years and their offspring need 12 years to reach sexual maturity. Baboons are post-menopausal for 5 years and need 5 years to reach sexual maturity. Lions are post-menopausal for 2 years and need 2 years to reach sexual maturity.

CHAPTER 9

MONOGYNISTIC LOVE

Type of Emotion:	conceptual reward
Conceptual Trigger:	" the woman I love is happy "
Mental Effect:	positive
Key Features:	activation requires strong visual/audible pleasure activation requires suddenly strong affection cannot be activated by more than one woman at a time cannot be activated by previous women cannot be activated by kin or friends the happier the woman, the stronger the effect has a duration of 42 months for each woman

Purpose

Monogynistic love encourages men to support the mother of their children.

Monogynistic love encourages social, not sexual monogyny. While monogynistic love does encourage men to support one woman, it does not discourage men from having sex with other women. Male infidelity does not jeopardize maternal post-natal care. Maternal love ensures that mothers will care for a man's children.

Activation

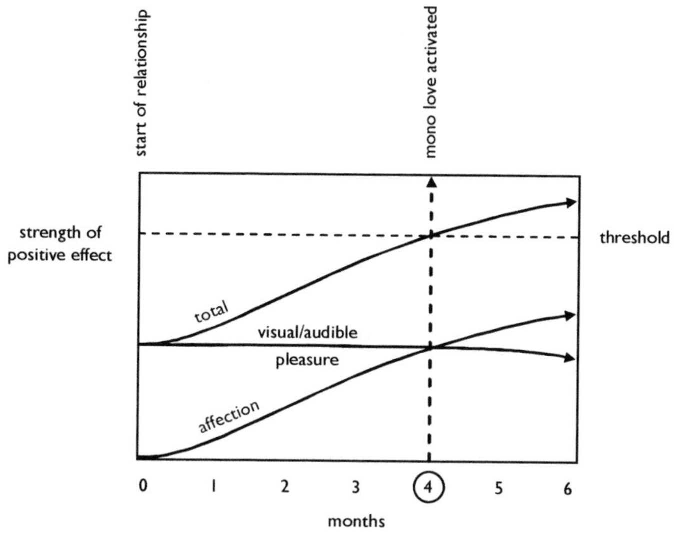

Monogynistic love is activated when the total of visual/audible pleasure and affection reaches a threshold. Activation specifically requires both strong visual/audible pleasure and suddenly strong affection within 4 months. Simply put, men fall in love when they interact with an attractive, new woman for 4 months.

Requiring strong visual/audible pleasure ensures fertility. Visual/audible pleasure is triggered by features that separate pre-menopausal, non-pregnant women from other humans. Protruding breasts and wide hips are two examples.

Requiring strong visual pleasure for 4 months ensures non-pregnancy prior to courtship. Strong visual pleasure is triggered by an hourglass figure: protruding breasts, narrow waist and wide hips. If a woman was impregnated by another man prior to courtship, she would lose her narrow waist and her hourglass figure by month 4.

Requiring suddenly strong affection ensures sexual exclusivity during courtship. To trigger strong affection in 4 months, a woman must spend most of her free time with a man. During this time, she would not have time to court another man.

Requiring suddenly strong affection also excludes previous women. Because they are familiar, previous women cannot trigger suddenly strong affection. This encourages men to change partners every reproductive cycle, which increases the genetic diversity of their offspring.

Requiring suddenly strong affection also excludes kin and friends. Because they are familiar, kin and friends cannot trigger suddenly strong affection. As a result, men can only fall in love with strangers.

Activation does not require copulation or pregnancy. Ideally, men would not fall in love until they copulated with and impregnated a woman. However, men cannot detect pregnancy until month 4 and monogynistic love needs to be activated at impregnation.

Monogynistic love cannot be activated by more than one woman at a time. This ensures that men focus their post-natal support on one woman.

Monogynistic love is disproportionately activated by women that look maternal. The more a woman looks like a man's mother, the stronger the affection she triggers in him. The stronger the affection a woman triggers in a man, the sooner she reaches his activation threshold. Simply put, men tend to fall in love with women with the same eye color, hair color, skin color and facial bone structure as their mothers. This encourages mating with compatible genes.

Conceptual Trigger

Monogynistic love is triggered by making a woman happy.

Before birth control, making a woman happy made a man's child happy. Women usually became pregnant when men fell in love.

With birth control, making a woman happy does not make a man's child happy. For childless women, maternal love is not the primary source of happiness. Instead, pride usually is. Pride is triggered by increased rank and diamond rings are a good way to increase rank. Diamond rings sales accelerated after the advent of the birth control pill in 1961.

Monogynistic love is triggered regardless of who makes a woman happy. Men feel love when their children make their woman happy, which avoids men competing with children for a mother's attention.

Mental Effect

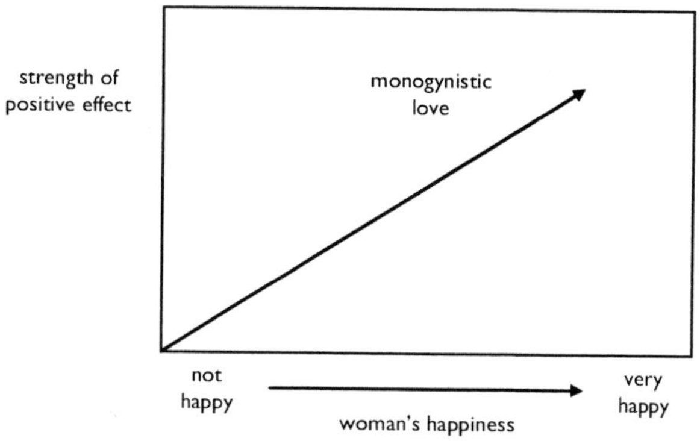

Monogynistic love varies with a woman's happiness. The happier a woman is, the stronger the positive effect. Men feel stronger love when they see their women smile.

Monogynistic love varies indirectly with a child's happiness. For women with children, maternal love is their primary source of happiness and it varies with a child's happiness.

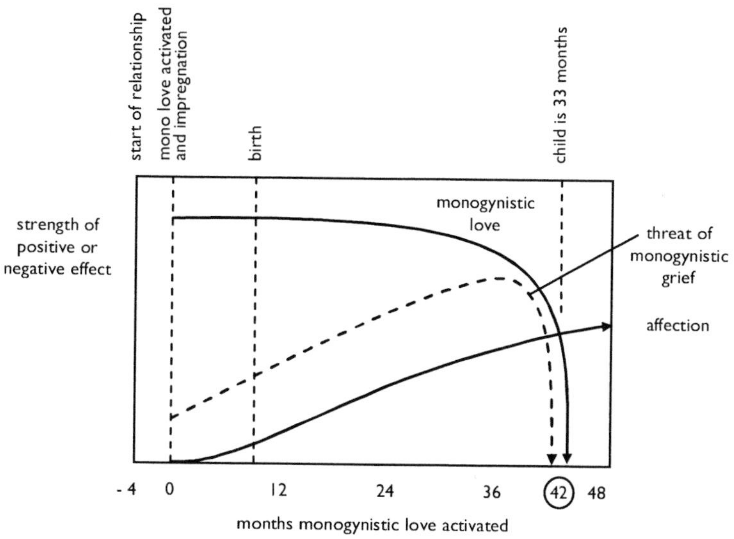

Monogynistic love has a duration of 42 months. Monogynistic love is usually activated after 4 months of courtship. Before birth control, the activation of monogynistic love usually coincided with impregnation. Monogynistic love stays active for 42 months to cover 9 months of gestation and 33 months of post-natal care. Monogynistic love ends when a child is 33 months old, concurrent with the end of maternal love. Both sexes maximize reproduction by starting a new reproductive cycle when a child can feed itself.

The threat of monogynistic grief also has a duration of 42 months.

Affection usually continues after monogynistic love ends.

Chapter 10

Monogynistic Grief

Type of Emotion:	conceptual punishment
Conceptual Trigger:	" the woman I love is dead "
Mental Effect:	negative
Key Features:	not triggered if monogynistic love is no longer active the longer love had been activated, the stronger the effect
Involuntary Expression:	prolonged frowning
Synonym:	sorrow

Purpose

Monogynistic grief encourages men to protect the mother of their children.

Conceptual Trigger

Monogynistic grief is not triggered if monogynistic love is no longer active. If a man fell in love with a woman more than 42 months ago, he will not feel grief if she dies. Men maximize their reproduction by moving onto a new woman after 42 months. Consequently, they are not punished for the death of a woman they should have left.

Monogynistic grief is triggered even if the dead woman was childless. Ideally, men would not be punished for the death of a childless woman. However, men cannot detect pregnancy before monogynistic love is activated.

Monogynistic grief is triggered by a woman's death, whether the man could have prevented it or not. This encourages men to treat all death as preventable.

Mental Effect

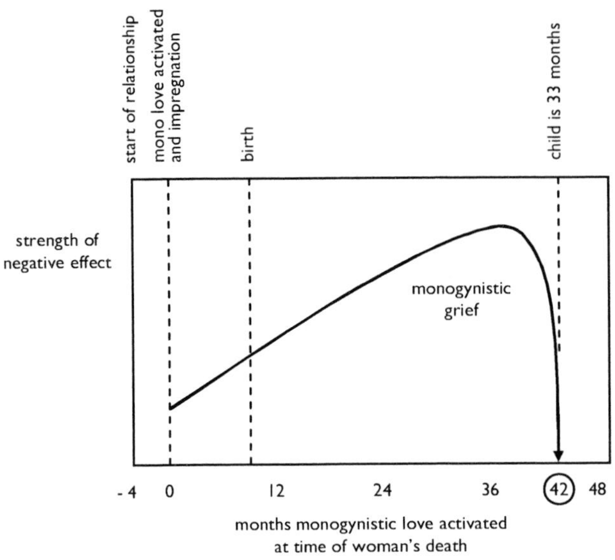

Monogynistic grief varies with the length of time monogynistic love had been activated. The longer a man had been in love with a woman when she dies, the stronger the negative effect. Men who had been in love for 42 months feel the strongest grief. Men who fell in love more than 42 months before a woman's death feel no grief.

Monogynistic grief varies with the man's investment. The more time has been invested, the more grief makes a man willing to protect his investment. A man is more likely to run into a burning building to save a woman he met 35 months ago than a woman he met 5 months ago.

Other Species

Other species feel monogynistic love and monogynistic grief. Marmoset monkeys, wolves and sand grouse are species where fathers help mothers with the feeding and protection of offspring.

Some species feel paternal love and paternal grief. Emperor penguins, rhea and sea horses are species where mothers leave fathers to feed and protect offspring.

Some species just feel paternal grief. Jacana, Darwin's frog and catfish are species where mothers leave fathers to protect, but not feed offspring.

Chapter 11

Other Types of Love

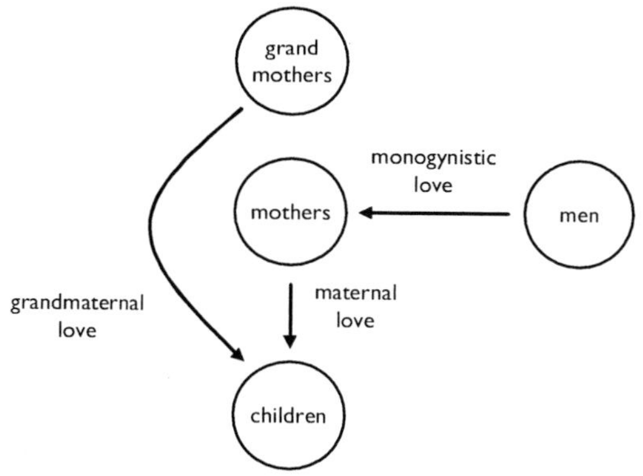

Only three people feel love. Mothers love children for 33 months. Grandmothers love grandchildren for 33 months. Men love women for 42 months.

Nobody else feels love. Women do not love men. Men do not love children. Children do not love parents, siblings or grandparents. Grandfathers do not love grandchildren. Friends do not love friends. People do not love pets.

Nobody else helps their genes by harming themselves to make another person happy, which is what love encourages you to do. Harming yourself to make another person happy only helps your genes if:

- you are a woman and the other person is your child or your grandchild
- you are a man and the other person is your child's mother

Other people feel infatuation, affection or cute. These positive effects are mistakenly believed to be love.

Women feel infatuation. Infatuation is triggered when a woman concludes that she triggers a man's visual/audible pleasure.

Everyone feels affection. Affection is triggered by the sight or sound of familiar people. Unlike love and infatuation, affection does not have a limited duration. Affection usually grows stronger with time.

Affection is what most people mean when they say they love somebody. Spouses feel affection after the end of monogynistic love and infatuation. Parents feel affection for children. Children feel affection for siblings, parents and grandparents. Grandparents feel affection for grandchildren. Friends feel affection for friends. People feel affection for pets.

Everyone older than 33 months feels cute. Cute is triggered by the sight of infants.

Chapter 12

Other Types of Grief

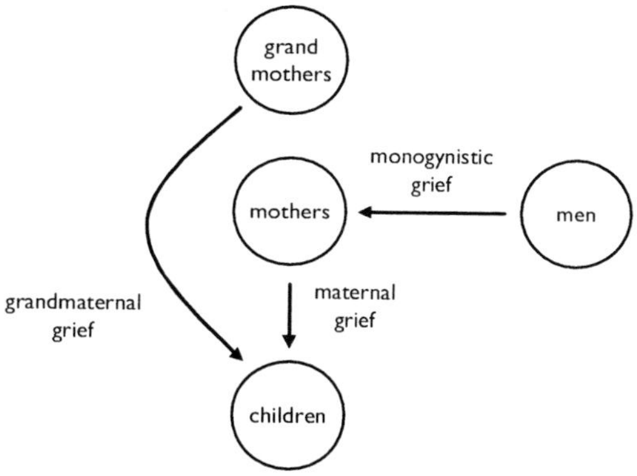

Only three people feel grief. Mothers feel grief when children die. Grandmothers feel grief when grandchildren die. Men in love feel grief when women die.

Nobody else feels grief when someone dies. Women do not feel grief when men die. Men do not feel grief when children die. Children do not feel grief when siblings, parents or grandparents die. Grandfathers do not feel grief when grandchildren die. Friends do not feel grief when friends die. People do not feel grief when pets die.

Nobody else helps their genes by harming themselves to protect another person, which is what grief encourages you to do. Harming yourself to protect another person only helps your genes if:

- you are a woman and the other person is your child or your grandchild
- you are a man and the other person is your child's mother

Other people feel loneliness when someone dies. This negative effect is mistakenly believed to be grief.

Loneliness is triggered by the absence of affection. When someone close to you dies, you imagine the absence of their affection. Imagining that absence triggers loneliness.

CHAPTER 13

INFATUATION

Type of Emotion:	conceptual reward
Conceptual Trigger:	" I trigger visual/audible pleasure in X, a man who displays group emotions as much as I do "
Mental Effect:	positive
Key Features:	has a duration of 8 months for each man grows stronger for 4 months and then plateaus for 4 months does not grow stronger without suddenly strong affection does not grow stronger for previous men does not grow stronger for kin or friends during plateau, vaginal pleasure is temporarily elevated the more group emotions displayed, the stronger the effect group emotions must be equal-or-stronger to the woman's not triggered during gestation and maternal love

Purpose

Infatuation encourages women to activate a man's monogynistic love.

	conceptions	sensations	reflexes	involuntary expressions	voluntary expressions
individual		pleasing taste, hunger, disgust	startle fear		
genetic	maternal love & grief grandmaternal love & grief monogynistic love & grief infatuation, heartbreak jealousy, adulterous guilt	sexual pleasure, lust, repugnance affection, cute, loneliness		horror momentary frowning prolonged frowning momentary smiling crying	
group	revenge, criminal guilt compassion, selfish guilt pride, humiliation humor, envy	excitement, boredom		prolonged smiling blushing	anger laughter

Infatuation also encourages women to prefer men who display group emotions.

Men who display group emotions are macho, law-abiding, brave, charitable, ambitious, funny and adventurous. Macho men feel revenge. Law-abiding men feel criminal guilt. Brave men feel compassion. Charitable men feel selfish guilt. Ambitious men feel pride, humiliation and envy. Funny men feel humor. Adventurous men feel excitement and boredom. A mensch is a man who displays strong group emotions.

Women often judge a man's group emotions by his rank. The higher a man's rank, the more he must be driven by group emotions.

The component of infatuation that encourages women to prefer men who display group emotions is labelled the group preference component.

	group emotions	share of population	share of reproduction time	share of offspring
men	above average	50 %	40 %	40 %
	below average	50 %	60 %	60 %
women	above average	50 %	40 %	40 %
	below average	50 %	60 %	60 %
men & women	above average	50 %	40 %	40 %
	below average	50 %	60 %	60 %

Without the group preference component, people with above-average group emotions would have disproportionately low reproduction. Because they spend more time helping their groups, people with above-average group emotions spend less time on reproduction. While they have a 50% share of the population, they may only have a 40% share of reproduction time. Without the group preference component, a 40% share of reproduction time translates into a 40% share of offspring.

If the group preference component did not exist, group emotions would not exist.

	group emotions	share of population	share of reproduction time	share of offspring
men	above average	50 %	40 %	60 %
	below average	50 %	60 %	40 %
women	above average	50 %	40 %	40 %
	below average	50 %	60 %	60 %
men & women	above average	50 %	40 %	50 %
	below average	50 %	60 %	50 %

With the group preference component, people with above-average group emotions have proportionate reproduction. With the group preference component, courtship is much easier for men with above-average group emotions. Their 40% share of reproduction time translates into a 60% share of offspring. Their 60% share combines with women's 40% share to give all people with above-average group emotions a 50% share of offspring. The additional children produced by male executives offsets the smaller-than-average families of female executives.

The group preference component preserves the group emotions.

Preferring men with above-average group emotions harms a woman's genes.

These men require more courtship time. There is more competition for men with above-average group emotions. Consequently, women must spend more time courting them. If women courted average men, they would have more time for children.

Their children do not live longer. Men with above-average group emotions can usually provide their children with more assets, like cell phones and cars. However, these assets do not help their children live longer.

Their children do not reproduce more. While their sons reproduce more, their daughters reproduce less. Combined, they have proportionate reproduction.

Male infatuation did not evolve.

Male infatuation is not required. Maternal love, the counterpart to monogynistic love, does not require activation.

Men do not spend money or time triggering infatuation. Men do not buy romance novels. Men rarely watch romantic movies unless they are with a woman.

Men do feel monogynistic love, affection and sexual pleasure when courting a woman. These positive effects are mistakenly believed to be male infatuation.

Conceptual Trigger

Infatuation is triggered when men look at or listen to a woman, not when they have sex with her. Infatuation rewards women for activating monogynistic love, which requires triggering a man's visual/audible pleasure, not his penile pleasure. Vaginal pleasure, which rewards women for tolerating copulation, is elevated when infatuation plateaus. Prior to the plateau, women enjoy dating more than sex. It triggers more infatuation.

Infatuation requires that group emotions displayed be equal-or-stronger to the woman's. For example, a woman does not feel infatuation unless a man's rank is equal-or-higher than her rank. Teenage girls enjoy construction workers whistling at them, but supermodels do not. Construction workers are higher rank for teenagers, but lower rank for supermodels.

Requiring equal-or-stronger group emotions eliminates most competitors. Men with below-average group emotions cannot trigger the infatuation of a woman with average group emotions.

Unlike monogynistic love, infatuation can be simultaneously triggered by multiple men. Men can only love one woman at a time, but women can be infatuated with more than one man at a time. This creates more competition between men.

Infatuation's trigger contains nothing to encourage the avoidance of lotharios. Heartbreak encourages the avoidance of lotharios. Because heartbreak addresses the lothario problem, infatuation's conceptual trigger has room to accommodate the group preference component.

Mental Effect

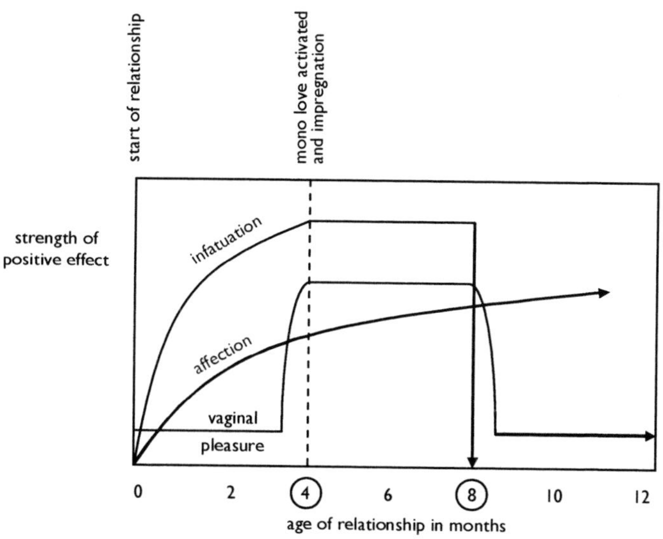

Infatuation has a duration of 8 months for each man.

During the first 4 months, infatuation grows stronger if one man keeps triggering it. This causes women to focus on one man, which they must do to trigger strong enough affection to activate monogynistic love.

During the second 4 months, infatuation plateaus and vaginal pleasure is elevated. Elevated vaginal pleasure encourages women to mate. During these 4 months, women almost enjoy sex as much as men do.

After a total of 8 months, infatuation stops and vaginal pleasure subsides. The plateau lasts 4 months to cover at least 3 ovulatory cycles. If a man cannot impregnate a woman in 3 cycles, he probably never will. After 4 months, infatuation stops and vaginal pleasure subsides.

After 8 months, women only feel affection for a man. After 8 months, women lose interest in triggering a man's visual/audible pleasure. They would rather talk, which triggers affection.

Infatuation does not grow stronger without suddenly strong affection within 4 months.

Requiring suddenly strong affection ensures the activation of monogynistic love. If a woman feels affection which grows suddenly strong within 4 months, the man must also feel suddenly strong affection. If he feels suddenly strong affection within 4 months, he has probably fallen in love.

Requiring suddenly strong affection prevents infatuation with previous men. Because they are familiar, men that have previously grown a woman's infatuation cannot trigger suddenly strong affection. This encourages women to change partners every reproductive cycle, which increases the genetic diversity of their offspring.

Requiring suddenly strong affection also prevents infatuation with kin or friends. Because they are familiar, kin and friends cannot trigger suddenly strong affection. As a result, women can only become infatuated with strangers.

Infatuation is disproportionately triggered by men that look maternal. The more a man looks like a woman's mother, the stronger the affection he triggers in her. The stronger the affection a man triggers in a woman, the sooner he reaches her infatuation plateau. Simply put, women tend to become infatuated with men that have the same eye color, hair color, skin color and facial bone structure as their mothers. This encourages mating with compatible genes.

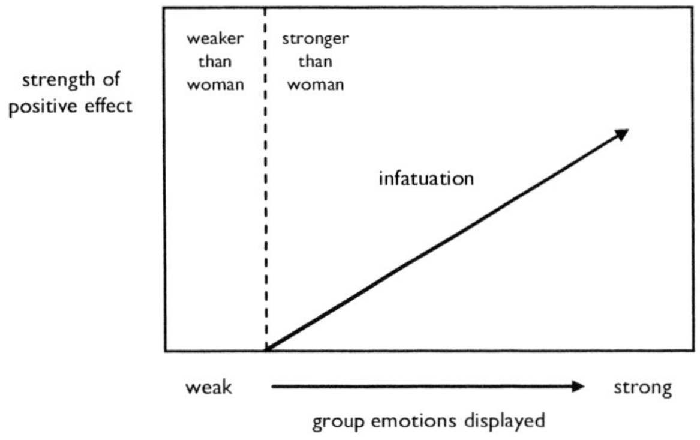

Infatuation also varies with group emotions displayed. The stronger a man's display of group emotions, the stronger the positive effect.

Rank is one measure of a man's group emotions. The higher a man's rank, the stronger the infatuation he triggers. Women prefer men who are rich, successful or intelligent because they trigger stronger infatuation.

High-ranking men have more sex because they can. High-ranking men do not have more sex because they have more desire. Men's desire for sex does not vary with their rank, but women's infatuation does. Women desire high-ranking men more.

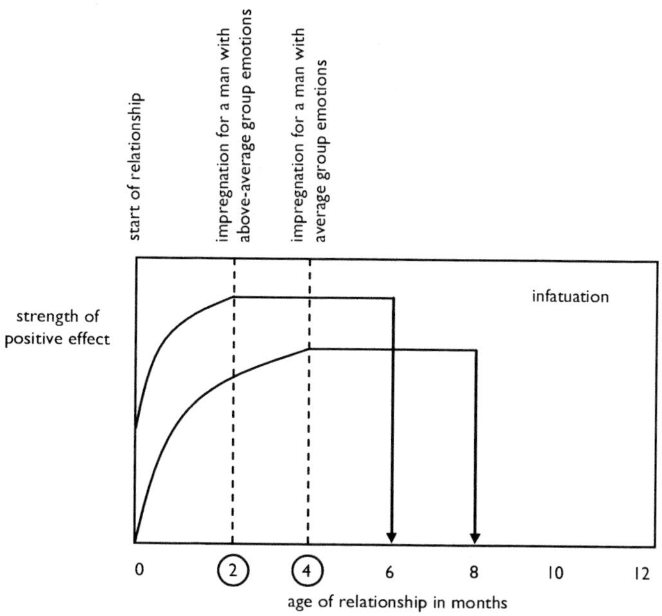

Men with above-average group emotions reach the infatuation plateau sooner. Because they trigger stronger starting infatuation, men with above-average group emotions start closer to the plateau. While an average man requires 4 months to reach the plateau, above-average men may only require 2 months.

Childless Relationships

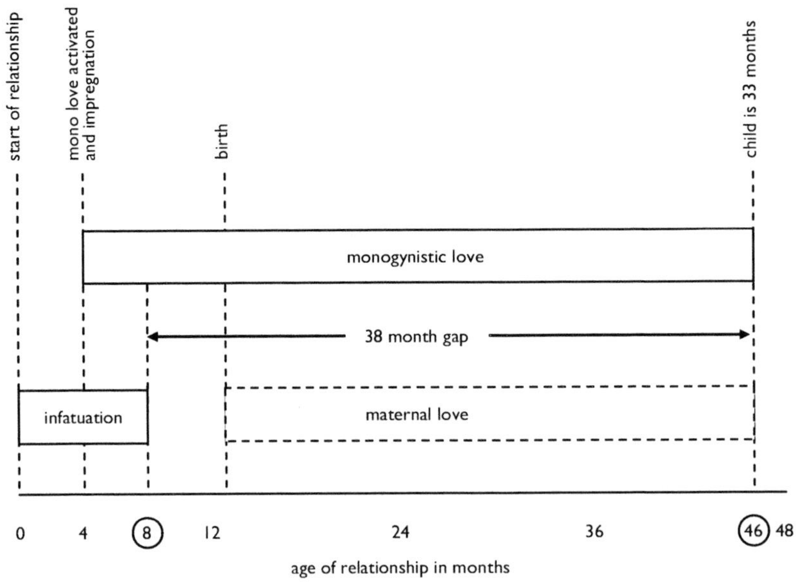

Childless relationships leave a 38 month gap for women.

Before birth control, both genders felt strong positive conceptions for almost 4 years. Men felt 42 months of monogynistic love. Women felt 8 months of infatuation, followed by a 5 month gap and then 33 months of maternal love.

With birth control, women do not feel maternal love from month 13 to 46. After infatuation ends, childless women only feel affection while men feel monogynistic love. During this 38 month gap, women often become focused on marriage, mistakenly believing that it will provide what seems to be missing in their lives.

Relationship Duration

Couples usually split 5 years after courtship begins. Neither gender feels a strong positive conception after 4 years. It then takes another year to realize and confront the fact that neither person feels passion anymore. The peak year for divorce is 4 years after marriage, as Helen Fisher identified in her book *The Anatomy of Love.*

CHAPTER 14

HEARTBREAK

Type of Emotion:	conceptual punishment
Conceptual Trigger:	" the man I am infatuated with wants to make another woman happy "
Mental Effect:	negative
Key Feature:	the stronger the infatuation, the stronger the effect

Purpose

Heartbreak encourages women to avoid lotharios. Lotharios are men who pretend to fall in love to have sex. Afterwards, they leave women to raise children without paternal support, a worst case scenario for a woman's genes.

Male heartbreak did not evolve. Female lotharios do not exist. Maternal love ensures that mothers care for a man's child.

Men may stop feeling love or start feeling jealousy or loneliness if a woman leaves. These reductions in happiness are mistakenly believed to be male heartbreak.

Men will stop feeling monogynistic love if they were still in love when a woman leaves. Without contact with the woman, a man cannot conclude that she is happy.

Men feel jealousy if they were in love and the woman leaves for another man.

Men feel loneliness if the woman was an important source of affection before she left.

Conceptual Trigger

Heartbreak is only triggered if a woman is still infatuated with a man. If a woman started feeling infatuation more than 8 months ago, she will not feel heartbreak if her man courts another woman. If she has not activated his monogynistic love after 8 months, she probably never will and should move on to a new man. Consequently, women are not punished for losing a man they should have left.

Heartbreak is triggered by making another woman happy, not by having sex with her. Women do not feel heartbreak if their man has sex with another woman. Women do feel heartbreak if their man buys another woman presents. Men have sex to make themselves happy. Men buy a woman presents to make her happy. If a man wants to make another woman happy, he is in love with her. If a man is in love with another woman, he cannot be in love with the heartbroken woman.

Imaginary heartbreak is more important than actual heartbreak. Actual heartbreak is triggered after a woman has been fooled by a lothario. Imaginary heartbreak is triggered before a woman is fooled by a lothario. It is easier for women to imagine heartbreak when they have felt it before. Lotharios target naive women for this reason.

Mental Effect

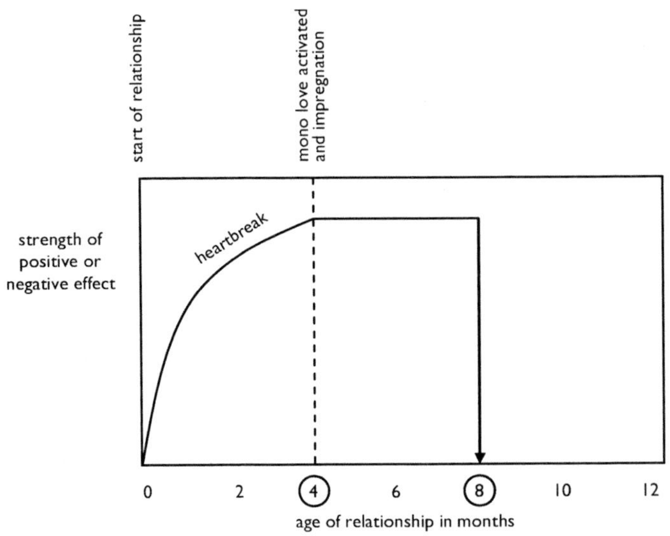

Heartbreak varies with a woman's infatuation. The stronger a woman's infatuation, the stronger the negative effect. Being heartbroken during the 4 month plateau triggers the strongest heartbreak. Being heartbroken after the plateau has ended triggers no effect.

Heartbreak varies with the risk of pregnancy, which is greatest during the 4 months that vaginal pleasure is elevated.

CHAPTER 15

JEALOUSY

Type of Emotion:	conceptual coercion
Conceptual Trigger:	" the woman I love made another man feel sexual pleasure "
Mental Effect:	negative
Conceptual Stop:	" I harmed the woman I love as much she made another man feel sexual pleasure "
Key Feature:	the stronger the other man's pleasure, the stronger the effect
Voluntary Expression:	anger
Synonym:	not envy

<u>Purpose</u>

Jealousy encourages men to punish female infidelity. Punishing female infidelity prevents men from mistakenly investing 42 months in another man's child, a worst case scenario for a man's genes.

Female jealousy did not evolve. Male infidelity cannot cause a woman to mistakenly invest in another woman's child. Princess Diana knew that her sons were hers. Prince Charles does not.

Women can feel humiliation, heartbreak and revenge if a man commits infidelity. These negative effects are mistakenly believed to be female jealousy.

Women feel humiliation if infidelity lowers their rank. If a woman is the last to know about her man's infidelity, it lowers her rank.

Women feel heartbreak if they were infatuated and the infidelity was more than sex. If a man buys another woman presents, he wants to make her happy. If he wants to make her happy, he loves her.

Women also feel revenge when humiliated or heartbroken. A woman's revenge is stopped by harming the man as much as she was harmed by humiliation or heartbreak.

Jealousy and revenge are different. Female infidelity causes men to feel jealousy, whether they feel humiliated or not. Male infidelity causes women to feel revenge, but only if they feel humiliated or heartbroken.

Conceptual Trigger

Jealousy can be triggered by any sexual pleasure, not just penile. Jealousy is triggered when another man enjoys visual pleasure while looking at a woman. This encourages men to punish the earliest stages of courtship. Punishing early courtship prevents escalation to sex. Punishing penile pleasure would be too late.

Jealousy is only triggered when monogynistic love is active. If a man fell in love more than 42 months ago, he will not feel jealousy if his woman flirts with another man. After 42 months, a man should be on a new reproductive cycle with a new woman.

Women often trigger jealousy to verify monogynistic love. Women intuitively know that a jealous man is a man in love. A woman will flirt with other men just to see if it triggers jealousy in her man. If it does, he must be in love.

Mental Effect

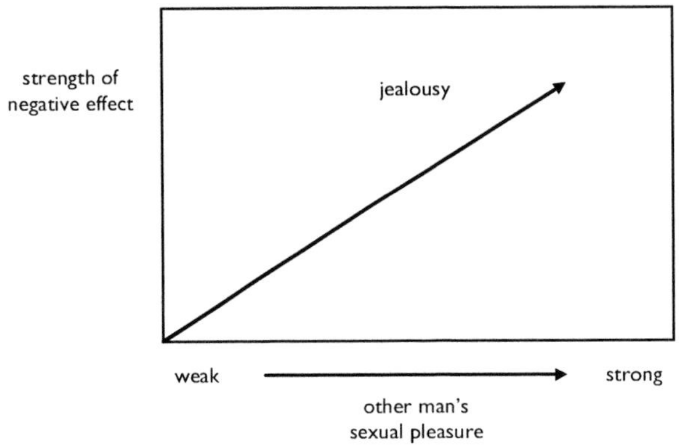

Jealousy varies with the other man's sexual pleasure. The stronger the other man's sexual pleasure, the stronger the negative effect A man will feel weak jealousy if another man looks at his woman. A man will feel much stronger jealousy if another man is fellated by his woman.

The strength of jealousy determines the likelihood of punishment. A man may tolerate another man just looking at his woman, but he will not tolerate another man being fellated by his woman.

While the strength of jealousy determines the likelihood of punishment, the wording of its conceptual stop determines how much a man punishes a woman.

Conceptual Stop

Jealousy is stopped by harm equal to the other man's pleasure. If a woman just flirted with another man, jealousy can be stopped by giving her the cold shoulder. If she fellated another man, jealousy may not be stopped until she is physically harmed.

Childless Relationships

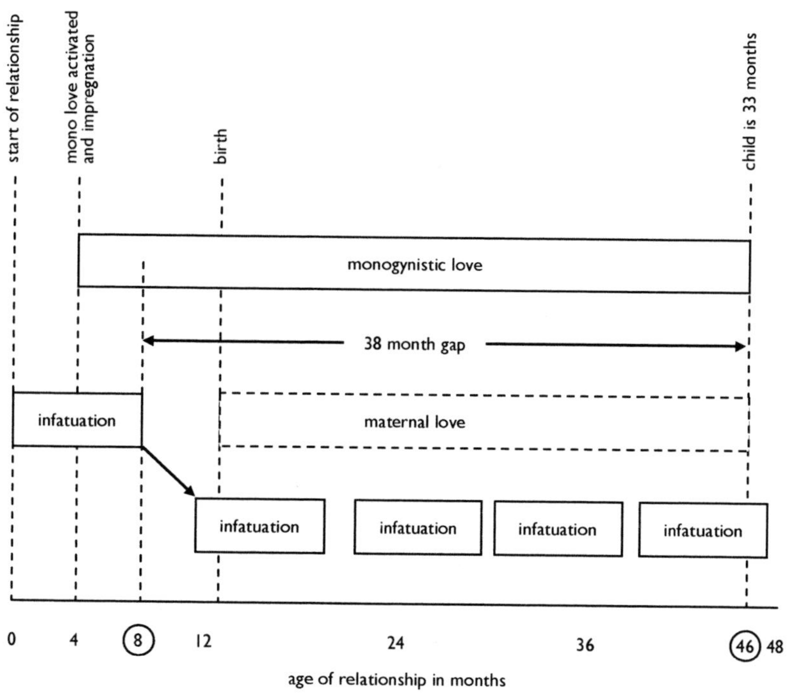

Jealousy is frequently triggered during the 38 month gap of childless relationships. Since women do not feel maternal love, they seek new men to trigger their infatuation. While women may not have sex with other men during this period, they will enjoy flirtation with other men, which triggers jealousy in the man that loves them.

Jealousy and Envy

	jealousy	envy
who	men in love	everyone
conceptual trigger	" my woman made another man feel sexual pleasure "	" X, a former peer, is now higher rank than me "
mental effect	negative	negative
conceptual stop	" I harmed my woman as much as she pleasured the other man "	

Jealousy and envy are not synonyms.

Jealousy can only affect men in love. Envy can affect everyone.

Jealousy and envy are triggered by different conclusions. Jealousy is triggered when women commit infidelity. Envy is triggered when a peer's rank rises above your rank.

Jealousy and envy are both negative mental effects.

Jealousy is stopped by punishing a philandering woman. Envy does not have a conceptual stop. Envy only stops when the conceptual trigger is no longer true. Either your rank rises to your peer's level or your peer's rank falls back to your level.

CHAPTER 16

ADULTEROUS GUILT

Type of Emotion:	conceptual punishment
Conceptual Trigger:	" I made a man feel sexual pleasure who is not the father of my child "
Mental Effect:	negative
Key Features:	only triggered during gestation and maternal love the stronger the other man's pleasure, the stronger the effect

Purpose

Adulterous guilt encourages mothers to avoid infidelity while their children are younger than 33 months.

Maternal infidelity can cause the loss of male post-natal support. Triggering a man's jealousy can cause a man to abandon a woman he loves, leaving her to raise a child without paternal support, a worst case scenario for a woman's genes.

Male adulterous guilt did not evolve. Male infidelity cannot harm a man's genes. Maternal love ensures that mothers care for a man's child, even if he commits infidelity.

Adulterous men may feel criminal guilt if they commit infidelity. This negative effect is mistakenly believed to me male adulterous guilt.

Men feel criminal guilt if their infidelity causes a woman to feel humiliation or heartbreak. If it causes neither, a man will not feel criminal guilt.

Adulterous guilt and criminal guilt are different. Infidelity causes mothers to feel adulterous guilt, whether their man feels humiliation or not. Infidelity causes men to feel criminal guilt, but only if their woman feels humiliation or heartbreak.

Conceptual Trigger

Adulterous guilt is only triggered during maternal love. Childless women and women with children older than 33 months do not feel adulterous guilt. Unless a woman is pregnant or has children younger than 33 months, she always maximizes her reproduction by courting numerous men until one starts falling in love with her. Consequently, non-maternal women are not punished for pleasuring another man.

Mental Effect

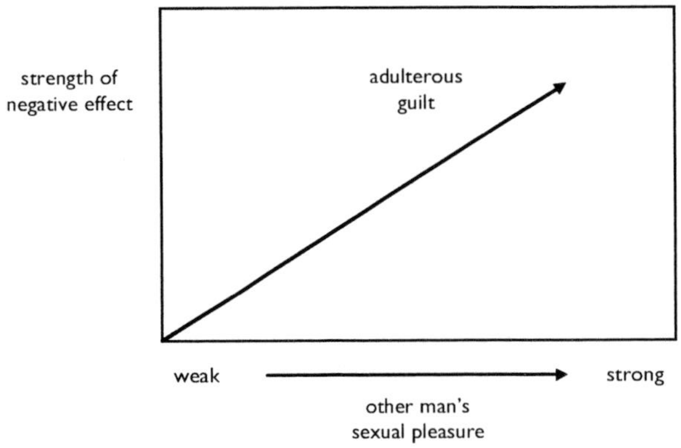

Adulterous guilt varies with jealousy. The more sexual pleasure the other man feels, the stronger the negative effect. A mother will feel weak adulterous guilt if she flirts with another man. A mother will feel stronger adulterous guilt if she fellates another man.

Adulterous guilt and jealousy both vary with the other man's sexual pleasure. Adulterous guilt is strong when jealousy is strong. This ensures that guilt increases its punishment as a woman increases the risk of losing male post-natal support.

CHAPTER 17
REVENGE

Type of Emotion:	conceptual coercion
Conceptual Trigger:	" X harmed me by breaking the rules "
Mental Effect:	negative
Conceptual Stop:	" I harmed X as much as X harmed me "
Key Features:	the more harm caused, the stronger the effect effect generally stronger in men
Voluntary Expression:	anger
Synonym:	hatred

Purpose

Revenge encourages victims of rule breaking to always retaliate, whether it helps them or not.

Rules include laws, by-laws, contracts, morals, protocol and etiquette.

Rules are a cultural adaptation that improve group efficiency. Rules force individuals to do what is best for a group when doing so is not what is best for the individual. Traffic flows more efficiently because we obey the rule that you stop at red lights.

Improving group efficiency helps group survival. The more efficiently a nation's traffic flows, the less it costs to feed its citizens.

Always retaliating deters rule breaking. People are less likely to break rules because they know that revenge is universal. Queues work because potential queue-jumpers expect retaliation from those waiting in the queue.

Always retaliating harms victims. Retaliating can help a victim, but always retaliating does not. Retaliating only helps a victim if it prevents future harm to that victim. If you are mugged by a neighbor, reporting it to the police helps you. You will reduce your risk of being mugged again. If you are mugged in a foreign city, reporting it to the police does not help you. You will not reduce your risk of being mugged again.

Always retaliating also harms a victim's genes. Reporting a mugging in a foreign city does not provide an offsetting benefit to your reproduction. However, reporting the mugging does help the survival and reproduction of the people who live in that city. Their risk of crime is reduced without any effort on their part.

"Revenge is a dish best served cold" refers to minimizing the harm that retaliating causes to a victim. If you retaliate when you are cool-headed, you can retaliate without breaking the rules and therefore avoid punishment and counter-retaliation.

Conceptual Trigger

Revenge is triggered when you are harmed by rule breaking.

Harm is anything which reduces happiness. Revenge is triggered by rule breaking that harms you physically, financially or emotionally. You feel revenge if somebody's rule breaking causes you to feel negative emotions, like grief or humiliation. You also feel revenge if somebody's rule breaking prevents you from feeling positive emotions, like affection or pride.

Revenge requires rule breaking. You feel revenge if another driver collides with your car because they were speeding. You do not feel revenge if another driver collides with your car because they swerved to avoid a child.

Revenge requires harm to you. Witnesses to rule breaking do not feel revenge. If revenge was triggered in victims and witnesses, there would be too much retaliation.

Mental Effect

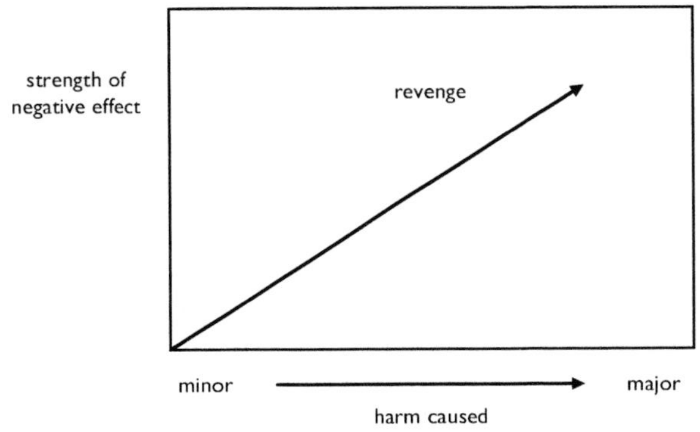

Revenge varies with the harm caused. The more harm caused to a victim, the stronger the negative effect. You will feel revenge if a mugger forces you to give up your wallet. You will feel stronger revenge if the mugger also breaks your nose.

The strength of revenge determines the likelihood of retaliation. You are more likely to report a violent mugger to the police than a non-violent mugger.

While the strength of revenge determines the likelihood of retaliation, the wording of its conceptual stop determines how much you retaliate.

Revenge is generally stronger in men. Given the same harm caused, men feel a stronger negative effect than women. Men fight more because they feel stronger revenge.

Revenge is stronger in men because male retaliation harms a group less. Because they are physically larger, men can punish rule breakers more easily than women. Men can punish both men and women. Women can only punish women.

Conceptual Stop

Stopping revenge requires equal harm or eye-for-an-eye punishment. The families of murder victims complain when murderers receive less than life imprisonment.

Stopping revenge requires victim participation. Numerous victims of a serial rapist will testify against the rapist, despite one being sufficient for a conviction. The victims know that they will not stop feeling revenge unless they participate in the conviction. Requiring victim participation ensures that equal harm is achieved when multiple victims are involved.

Apologies, anger and violence stop revenge.

Receiving an apology stops revenge without causing physical harm. If somebody apologizes to you, they have admitted to being a rule breaker. They have lowered their rank, which triggers their humiliation. Seeing an apologist feel humiliation is equal harm for minor rule breaking, like being late for a meeting.

Expressing anger also stops revenge without causing physical harm. If you express anger, you are threatening to harm someone. If your threat is credible, you will trigger their fear. Triggering someone's fear is equal harm for moderate rule breaking, like rude driving.

Being violent stops revenge by causing physical harm. Victims resort to violence when expressing anger fails to frighten a rule breaker. Road rage often escalates to violence when a victim of rude driving expresses anger at a rude driver and the rude driver responds by laughing. The laughing triggers the victim's humiliation, further adding to their revenge.

Revenge accumulates if not stopped. The negative effect of revenge does not fade away if it is not stopped. It accumulates and re-emerges later, usually in a disproportionate response to minor rule breaking. Men often respond disproportionately to minor rule breaking by family members after accumulating revenge all day at work.

Forgiveness is living with unstopped revenge. If you forgive someone, you are stating that you will not retaliate to stop your revenge. Instead, you will live with the negative effect, hoping that it will fade away with time. It is easy to forgive rule breaking that is ambiguous and causes minor harm, such as minor property damage caused by carelessness. It is more difficult to forgive rule breaking that is unambiguous and causes major harm, such as violence that causes injury.

Forgiveness does not stop revenge. Unstopped revenge does not fade away, regardless of the ambiguity of the rule breaking or the harm caused. If you think you were harmed by rule breaking, you will feel revenge until you retaliate. If you forgive someone, you will stop your revenge by subconsciously retaliating against the rule breaker or by harming a different person. Children retaliate against cruel parents by spending less time with them in old age. Wives with cruel husbands harm their children.

Other Species

Tamarin monkeys feel revenge. Experimenters trained one monkey to always cheat when playing a game with other monkeys. Victims of the cheater "would go nuts" when they saw the cheater enter the adjoining test chamber. Victims "would throw their feces at the wall, walk into the corner and sit on their hands". The victim reaction was reported by Stephen Dubner and Steven Levitt in *Monkey Business (The New York Times)*. The experiments, led by Marc Hauser and Keith Chen, are summarized in *Give Unto Others: Genetically Unrelated Cotton-Top Tamarin Monkeys Preferentially Give Food to Those Who Altruistically Give Food Back (Proceedings of The Royal Society)*.

Chapter 18

Criminal Guilt

Type of Emotion:	conceptual punishment
Conceptual Trigger:	" I harmed X by breaking the rules "
Mental Effect:	negative
Key Features:	the more harm caused, the stronger the effect effect generally stronger in men

Purpose

	method of reducing rule breaking	people who bear the cost
highest cost	obstacles	everybody
↑	retaliation (revenge)	victim and rule breaker
lowest cost	criminal guilt	nobody

Criminal guilt encourages everyone to avoid rule breaking.

Criminal guilt is the lowest cost method of reducing rule breaking. Criminal guilt costs your group nothing. Nobody is physically harmed and no expense is incurred.

Retaliation costs more than criminal guilt. Revenge causes retaliation, which harms both the victim and the rule breaker. A victim cannot work while participating in conviction of a criminal. A criminal does not work while incarcerated.

Obstacles are the highest cost. Obstacles include locks, bulletproof glass, security guards and the police. Everyone pays for obstacles, not just victims and rule breakers. Billions of doors are locked and unlocked everyday to stop theft.

Criminal guilt is used where it is sufficient. Criminal guilt is usually sufficient to cause diners to leave tips in restaurants.

If criminal guilt is not sufficient, retaliation is added. Returning diners tip more. Returning diners want to avoid criminal guilt and retaliation by waiters.

If criminal guilt and retaliation are insufficient, obstacles are added. Tourist restaurants often have a mandatory service charge. If you do not pay it, the police will be called.

Criminal guilt harms potential rule breakers and their genes. You do not live longer or have more children because you tip. The waiter does.

Conceptual Trigger

Criminal guilt is triggered when you harm someone by breaking the rules.

Criminal guilt requires rule breaking. You will feel criminal guilt if your car hits a cyclist after you drive through a red light. You will not feel criminal guilt if your car hits a cyclist after the cyclist rides through a red light.

Criminal guilt requires harm to a victim. Criminals who commit victimless crimes, such as prostitutes and pot smokers, do not feel criminal guilt.

Mental Effect

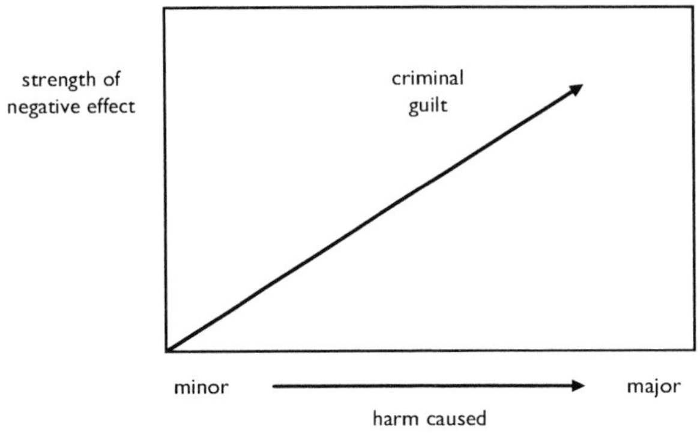

Criminal guilt varies with the harm caused. The more harm caused to a victim, the stronger the negative effect. Stealing $100 from a poor man triggers stronger criminal guilt than stealing $100 from a rich man.

Criminal guilt varies with the harm caused to reduce it. Rule breakers minimize their harm to minimize the guilt they feel. Thieves avoid stealing from the poor.

Modern justice systems graduate punishment in the same manner. If all criminals received the death penalty, all criminals would kill to avoid capture.

The police know that criminal guilt varies with the harm caused. When they have not caught a murderer, they will parade the murder victim's grieving mother in front of the news cameras. They want to increase the strength of the murderer's criminal guilt.

Confessing or being punished does not stop criminal guilt. All conceptual punishments are lifelong to ensure that you never forget the learning.

Criminal guilt is generally stronger in men. Given the same harm caused, men feel a stronger negative effect than women. Criminal guilt is more likely to drive men to commit suicide.

Criminal guilt is stronger in men because male rule breaking was more likely to cause death. If a man did not defend his perimeter during an attack, it could let the attackers flood into a fortification and kill all. If a woman took more than her share of food, others were unlikely to die as a result.

Other Species

Capuchin monkeys feel criminal guilt. An experiment required two monkeys to simultaneously pull two parts of a mechanism to receive one reward each. In one instance, only one monkey was able to retrieve his reward before they both let the spring-loaded mechanism pull away. This left one monkey with a reward and one without a reward. The monkey with a reward helped the monkey without a reward pull the mechanism again so that he could retrieve the remaining reward. He did this despite not receiving another reward. *Payment for Labour in Monkeys (Nature)* is the article that summarizes the experiments led by Frans de Waal and Michelle Berger.

In addition to criminal guilt, the altruistic monkey may have also felt compassion. The altruistic monkey would have felt compassion if it believed the other monkey was unfortunate, as described in the next chapter.

CHAPTER 19

COMPASSION

Type of Emotion:	conceptual coercion
Conceptual Trigger:	" I can prevent harm to an unfortunate person "
Mental Effect:	negative
Conceptual Stop:	" I prevented harm to an unfortunate person "
Key Features:	the more preventable harm, the stronger the effect effect generally stronger in women

Purpose

Compassion encourages everyone to help the unfortunate.

Helping the unfortunate saves lives. Helping strangers whose homes have burned down prevents them from dying of exposure or starvation. Calling an ambulance for a stranger who has fallen unconscious prevents that person from suffering further injury.

Helping the unfortunate also lowers the cost of insurance. Without compassion, you would need two of everything. You would need a second home, stocked with food and clothes. You could not count on your neighbors to help you if your first home burned down. You would also need to take a buddy everywhere. You could not count on strangers to call an ambulance if you fell unconscious.

Lowering the cost of insurance is more important more than saving lives. Saving lives affects a small percentage of a group. Lowering the cost of insurance affects everyone.

Conceptual Trigger

Compassion is triggered when you can prevent harm to an unfortunate person.

Harm is anything which reduces happiness. You feel compassion when you see somebody fall to the ground because of illness. You also feel compassion when you see somebody humiliated because of their race.

Compassion requires misfortune. You feel compassion when you see a double-amputee begging for change. You do not feel compassion when you see an able-bodied man begging for change.

If compassion did not require misfortune, it would reduce group survival. Everyone would feel compassion whenever someone asked for money. The streets would be lined with able-bodied beggars.

Compassion requires that you can prevent harm. You feel compassion if you see somebody fall to the ground in front of you. You do not feel compassion if you see somebody fall to the ground on *America's Funniest Home Videos*. You cannot prevent harm to the videotaped person. Instead, you feel humor.

Compassion can be mistakenly triggered by other species. You feel compassion when you see a dog hit by a car. Compassion is mistakenly triggered because you misinterpret "prevent harm to an unfortunate <u>person</u>" as "prevent harm to an unfortunate <u>animal</u>".

The more a species looks human, the more they mistakenly trigger compassion.

Animals with forward-facing eyes trigger compassion more than animals with side-facing eyes. Lions trigger more compassion than gazelles.

Animals with limbs trigger compassion more than animals without limbs. Gazelles trigger more compassion than fish.

Plants never trigger compassion. We kill trees just to decorate our houses for a week.

<u>Mental Effect</u>

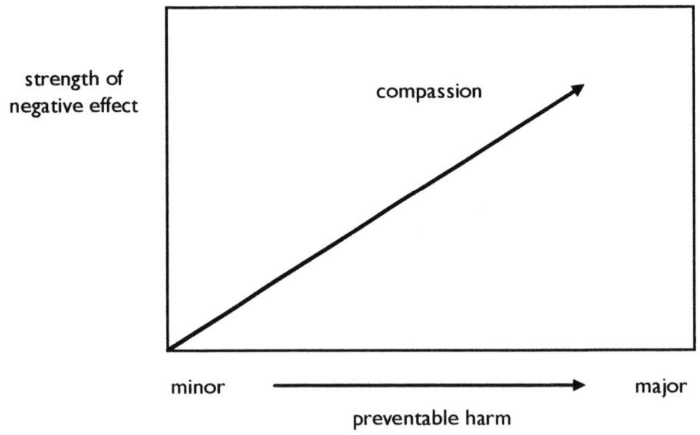

Compassion varies with the preventable harm. The more harm you can prevent, the stronger the negative effect. You would feel compassion if you saw an elderly man in a burning house. You would feel stronger compassion if you saw a young child in a burning house. Saving the young child would prevent the loss of more years of life.

Compassion varies to increase the likelihood of helping. Stronger compassion makes you more willing to rescue a young child than an elderly man.

While the strength of compassion determines the likelihood of helping, the wording of its conceptual stop determines how much you help.

Compassion does not vary with the number of unfortunate people. Compassion is triggered by one person at a time. You do not feel more compassion if many people are involved in a tragedy. Charities have learned this. They focus on unfortunate individuals when raising funds, not on the number of unfortunate.

Conceptual Stop

Compassion stops when no further harm can occur. Simply put, compassion stops when an unfortunate person is safe. If you rescue an unconscious child from a burning house, your compassion will continue if you lay the child on the ground and walk away. Your compassion will not stop until emergency workers are caring for the child.

You feel neutral when compassion stops. Heroes do not feel a positive effect after rescuing somebody. They just stop feeling the negative effect of compassion, unless they start talking to the media. Then they start feeling pride.

Other Species

Mammals that live in groups feel compassion.

Vampire bats feel compassion. Vampire bats do not always find a host every night. If they do not find a host, they may die before the next night. When bats return to the cave and find a starving neighbor, they will often regurgitate blood to feed their neighbor, whether the neighbor is kin or not.

Dolphins can feel compassion mistakenly triggered by another species. In New Zealand, a pod of dolphins protected a group of swimmers from a great white shark that was stalking them. The dolphins stayed between the swimmers and the circling shark until the swimmers reached safety. As reported in *Dolphins Prevent NZ Shark Attack (BBC News)*, marine biologists say such altruistic behavior is common in dolphins.

Bonobos can also feel compassion mistakenly triggered by another species. Frans de Waal reports the following in his book *Our Inner Ape:*

> " . . . consider a zoo bonobo named Kuni. When she saw a starling hit the glass of her enclosure, she picked up the stunned bird and climbed to the top of the tallest tree. She carefully unfolded its wings and spread them wide, holding one wing between the fingers of each hand, before sending the bird like a little toy airplane out towards the barrier of her enclosure. But the bird fell short of freedom and landed on the bank of the moat. Kuni climbed down and stood watch over the starling for a long time. By the end of the day, the recovered bird had flown off safely."

CHAPTER 20

SELFISH GUILT

Type of Emotion:	conceptual punishment
Conceptual Trigger:	" I failed to prevent harm to an unfortunate person "
Mental Effect:	negative
Key Features:	the more preventable harm, the stronger the effect effect generally stronger in women

Purpose

Selfish guilt encourages everyone to not wait for others to help the unfortunate.

Without selfish guilt, people would wait for others to help the unfortunate. When someone else helped an unfortunate person, you would stop feeling compassion without being harmed.

With selfish guilt, people who wait do not escape feeling a negative effect. If you let another person help an unfortunate person, you will start feeling selfish guilt when you stop feeling compassion.

Charities make it easier to stop compassion or avoid selfish guilt. You just pick up the phone and make a donation. Before charities, you had to visit unfortunate people to help them.

Commercial insurance is an alternative to compassion and selfish guilt. Both systems give large amounts to a few unfortunate people by taking small amounts from many fortunate people.

Conceptual Trigger

Selfish guilt is not triggered unless you could have prevented harm. Beggars do not feel selfish guilt saying no to another beggar.

Selfish guilt is not triggered unless the other person suffered misfortune. You do not feel selfish guilt saying no to an able-bodied beggar.

If selfish guilt did not require misfortune, it would harm group survival. Everyone would feel selfish guilt whenever they said no to a request for money. The streets would be lined with able-bodied beggars.

Selfish guilt can be mistakenly triggered by other species. You would feel selfish guilt if you left an animal writhing in pain.

Mental Effect

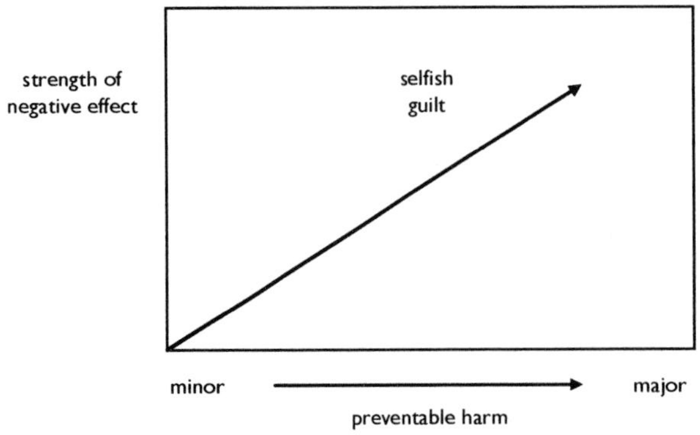

Selfish guilt varies with the preventable harm. The more harm you could have prevented, the stronger the negative effect. You will feel selfish guilt if you drive by a stranded motorist gesturing for help. You will feel stronger selfish guilt if the motorist dies of exposure that night.

Selfish guilt varies with preventable harm to increase the likelihood of helping next time. The stronger selfish guilt is, the more likely you will help in the future. If you have passed a stranded motorist that died, you are more likely to help stranded motorists in the future.

Compassion and selfish guilt are generally stronger in women. The difference is evident in voting and volunteering. Women are more inclined to vote for the left. Most volunteers are women.

Compassion and selfish guilt are stronger in women because they spend more time with children. Children are more likely to suffer misfortune. Also, rescuing a child saves more years of life than rescuing an adult.

Compassion and selfish guilt are the only group emotions that are stronger in women.

CHAPTER 21

PRIDE

Type of Emotion:	conceptual reward
Conceptual Trigger:	" my rank has increased "
Mental Effect:	positive
Key Features:	the larger the increase, the stronger the effect effect generally stronger in men
Involuntary Expression:	prolonged smiling
Synonym:	elation

Purpose

Pride encourages everyone to increase their rank.

Your rank reflects your contribution to group happiness. Your rank increases when you are expected to contribute more to your group's happiness. The unemployed increase their rank when they become employed.

Contributing more to group happiness helps group survival. The fewer unemployed there are, the more efficient a nation is.

Rank reflects expected future contributions to group happiness, not past contributions. Current presidents are higher rank than past presidents.

Rank is usually assigned with money. The more you contribute to group happiness, the more you are paid.

Rank is also assigned with titles, perquisites and trophies. High-ranking people are introduced as the honorable or chief executive. They are given large offices and parking spots near the door. They receive gold medals and statuettes.

Rank and pecking order are different.

Pecking order helps individuals by reducing competition. Pecking order sets a group's eating order to avoid having a fight before every meal. A pack of dogs avoids fighting before every meal by letting the top dog eat first and so on.

Rank harms individuals by increasing competition. Increasing your rank requires contributing more to group happiness than others. The more you contribute to your group's happiness, the more you harm yourself.

The harm caused by increasing rank can be seen in the early deaths of early leaders. Analysis of 1672 US governors by Stewart McCann showed that the younger a governor was when first elected, the sooner he died. The results are summarized in *Younger Achievement Age Predicts Shorter Life for Governors: Testing the Precocity-Longevity Hypothesis with Artifact Controls.* As reported in *The New York Times Magazine – The 3rd Annual Year in Ideas: Young Success Means Early Death,* the analysis produced the same result for Academy Award winners, Nobel laureates, prime ministers, presidents and pontiffs.

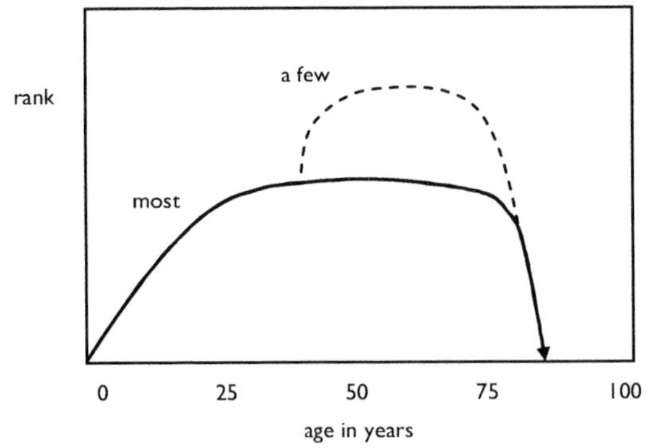

Rank is increased by learning or innovating.

Learning increases rank throughout childhood. During the first 20 years of life, your rank keeps increasing as you graduate to the next grade or school. Your rank continues to increase during the next 5 to 10 years of work as you learn new skills.

For most adults, rank plateaus in their thirties and remains unchanged until their seventies, when it declines with health.

For a few adults, innovating increases their rank. Dr. Steven Trokel was not content to run a successful ophthalmology practice in New York City. He went on to develop and patent the use of the Excimer laser for corrective eye surgery in 1992.

People usually regret not recognizing the importance of rank early in life. If they did, they would have invested more to increase their rank. Instead, many people push their children to avoid making the same mistake.

<u>Conceptual Trigger</u>

Pride is usually triggered when you:

- graduate from school
- win an award or contest
- are complimented by others
- receive a job offer, promotion or raise
- are the underdog and win
- are the favorite and win by more than the spread
- are treated as an equal by a higher-ranking person
- are first asked for your autograph
- buy or receive new possessions

Pride is triggered by higher rank, not high rank. Rookies feel pride, but veteran all-stars do not. Recent nursing graduates feel pride, but doctors nearing retirement do not.

	high rank	higher rank
top	✗	✗
nearly-top	✓	✓
above middle	✗	✓
middle	✗	✓
below middle	✗	✓
nearly-bottom	✗	✓
bottom	✗	✓

✗ not motivated

✓ motivated

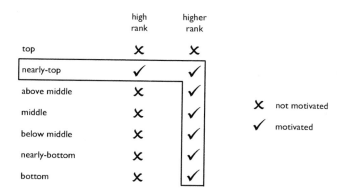

If pride was triggered by high rank, it would only motivate the nearly-top ranked. The top rank would not be motivated to increase their rank. They would feel pride just by maintaining their rank. The nearly-top ranked would be motivated. They would feel pride if they increased their rank. Ranks below the nearly-top rank would not be motivated. They would not feel pride if they increased their rank to the next level.

Because pride is triggered by higher rank, it motivates everyone below the top rank. Everyone below the top rank feels pride when they increase their rank. Vice-presidents feel pride when they are promoted to president. The unemployed feel pride when they become janitors.

By definition, pride is temporary. Pride is only triggered while you conclude that your rank is higher. Eventually, your higher rank is not higher anymore. A new car triggers pride for less than a year.

Pride is not triggered by slower growth. You will not feel pride if you receive a 5% salary increase and others receive a 10% salary increase. Pride only rewards improvements in relative contribution, which requires learning or innovation.

Pride is triggered by slower decline. You will feel pride if you receive a 5% salary rollback and others receive a 10% salary rollback. Rewarding slower decline encourages innovation during bad times.

Underdogs always feel pride when they win. Underdogs are not expected to win. Winning increases their rank.

Underdogs can also trigger pride if they lose by less than the spread. Underdogs are expected to lose by the spread. Losing by less than the spread increases their rank.

Favorites only feel pride if they win by more than the spread. Favorites are expected to win by the spread. They only increase their rank if they win by more than the spread.

Pride is triggered more frequently in growing companies. Their employees feel more pride because they are promoted more frequently than stagnant companies. Growing companies are more profitable because their employees feel more pride.

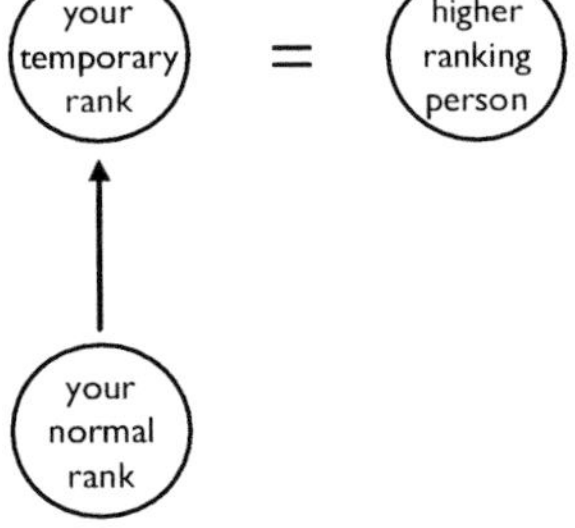

Being treated as an equal by a higher-ranking person triggers pride. If a higher-ranking person treats you as an equal, it feels like your rank has risen to their higher level. This happens when you meet a famous person.

High-ranking people, like royalty, know they have this effect on lower-ranking people. They know that investing a few minutes being down-to-earth with ordinary people leaves them with a strong positive memory. Afterwards, those ordinary people tell many friends and family how likeable the high-ranking person is.

Being complimented triggers pride. You feel pride the first few times someone says you are attractive or intelligent. Eventually, compliments from that person do not increase your rank further and therefore stop triggering pride.

Being asked for your autograph triggers pride for the first few months. People feel pride when strangers first ask for their autograph. The requests increase their rank to that of a famous person. After a few months, the requests stop triggering pride because they no longer increase the rank of the now-famous person.

New possessions usually trigger pride. New possessions are one of the ways we signal higher rank to others. The more your possessions cost, the higher your rank. Men often use cars to signal higher rank. Women often use clothes or jewelry.

People buy lottery tickets to help trigger imagined pride. People buy $10 lottery tickets despite knowing that the expected payoff is $6, for a net loss of $4 a ticket. However, that payoff does not include the benefit of imagined pride. Ticketholders can more credibly imagine winning than non-ticketholders. Their imagined pride is worth more than $4 a ticket.

Video games have many levels to trigger continuous pride. Each time a player reaches a new level or rank, they feel a burst of pride. Higher rank is recognized with audio/visual effects and awards, such as new weapons or privileges. Gamers become addicted to those bursts of pride, like drug users to heroin or gamblers to slot machines.

People seek challenges to trigger pride. A challenge is something which is a stretch for someone, meaning it requires increasing their rank. People usually seek alternative challenges when their career rank plateaus in their thirties. They start to collect things, run marathons or become politically active.

A sense of accomplishment is pride. If you had a particularly good week at work, you believe that your rank has increased.

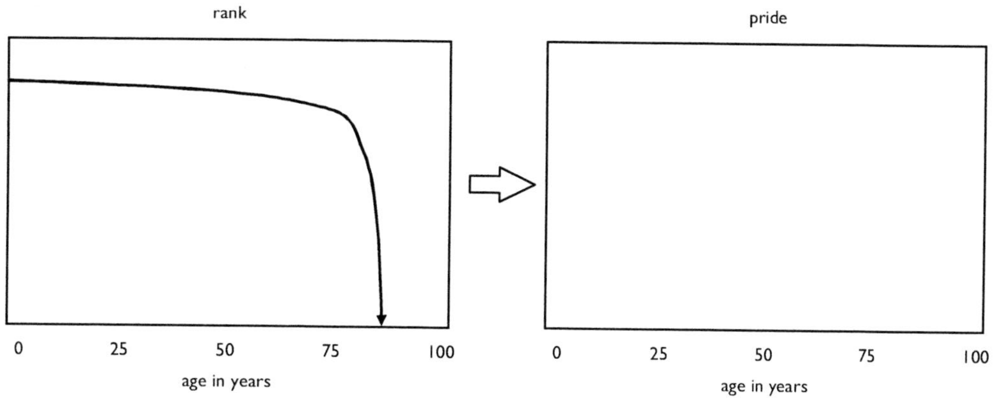

Rich children rarely feel pride. Rich children are born high rank and usually stay that way until their seventies. Because they start high rank, they rarely increase their rank. Their inability to feel pride makes them more dysfunctional than average.

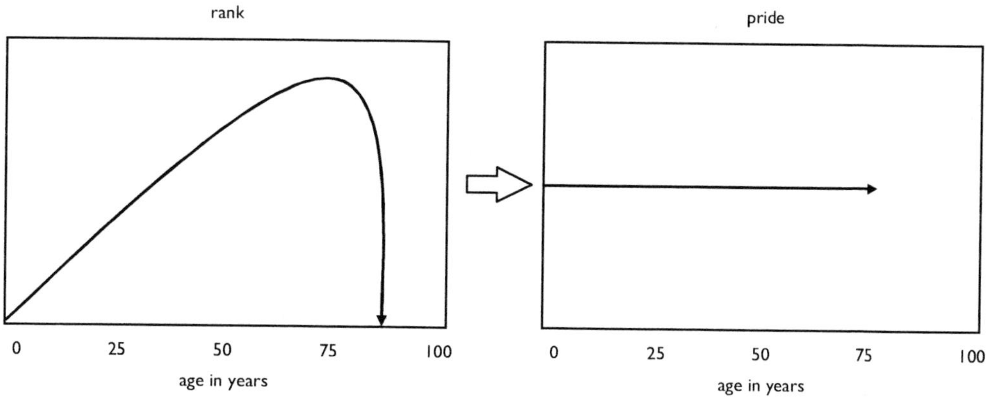

A rags-to-riches story is the best life plan. A continuous climb triggers continuous pride. Continuously increasing your rank for a lifetime requires starting at the bottom. If you start higher than the bottom, your rank will hit a plateau before death.

People trigger imagined pride to achieve rank increases that require long-term investment. To remain motivated through a project which only increases rank after many years, people often imagine the pride they will feel when the project is completed. To stay motivated while writing this book, I frequently imagined the pride I would feel when it was completed.

Imagined pride motivates people more than actual pride. Actual pride is triggered after someone increases their rank. Imagined pride is triggered when people are considering making the extra effort required to increase their rank. The prolonged smiling triggered by pride helps others imagine pride's positive effect.

Mental Effect

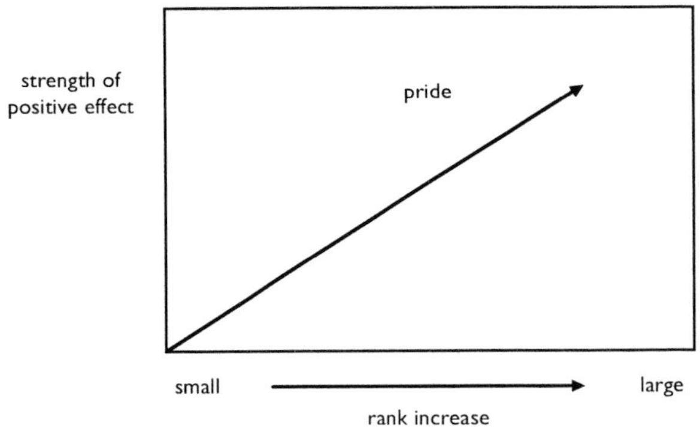

Pride varies with the rank increase. The larger the increase, the stronger the positive effect. Winning a million dollars triggers more pride in a beggar than a billionaire.

Pride varies with the rank increase to focus you where you can best contribute to group happiness. You pursue the career path that offers the greatest potential to increase your rank and therefore group happiness. Most lawyers become lawyers for the potential increase in rank, not to be stuck inside office buildings for long hours.

Pride is generally stronger in men. For the same increase in rank, men feel a stronger positive effect than women. The gender difference is evident in recreational choices. When men have recreational time, they compete or produce visible achievement. When women have recreational time, they socialize. Women prefer socializing because it triggers affection, which is stronger in women.

All four rank conceptions are stronger in men: pride, humiliation, humor and envy.

Rank emotions are stronger in men because lost male reproduction harms a group less. The higher your rank, the more you are contributing to your group. The more you contribute to your group, the less time you spend on reproduction. Lost male reproduction is offset by giving men courtship advantage through infatuation's group preference component and by increasing other men's reproduction. Lost female reproduction cannot be offset with courtship advantages or by increasing other women's reproduction.

Women cooperate more than men because their rank emotions are weaker. They are better team players because they seek pride and humor less than men. They enjoy the spotlight and humiliating others less than men. Women also seek humiliation and envy less. They are less likely to be offended by others or by unequal treatment.

Men compete more than women because their rank emotions are stronger.

All four rank emotions seem to grow stronger with age. They seem to play a more dominant role in your thoughts as you age. However, the strength of their mental effects does not change as you age. What changes is your awareness of their importance to your happiness.

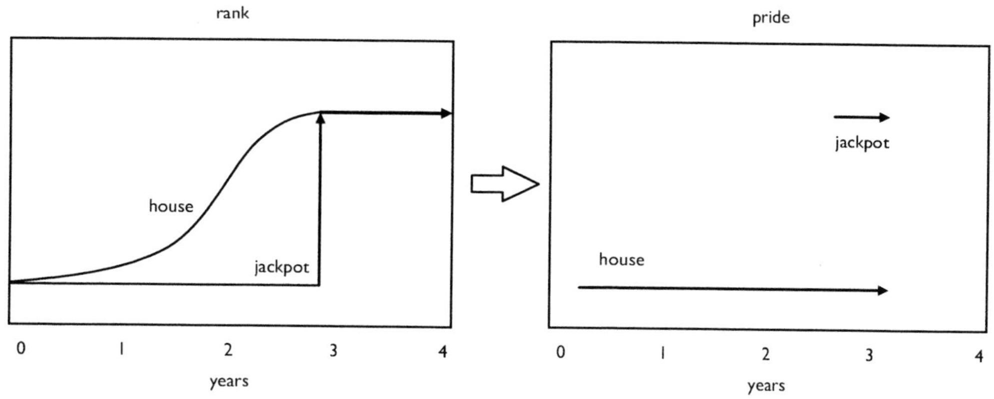

Gambling triggers very strong pride for a short time.

Winning a jackpot gives winners a large and sudden increase in rank. The probability of winning a jackpot is close to 0% moments before it happens. Winning causes the probability to instantly hit 100% and the gambler's rank to skyrocket. As their rank skyrockets, gamblers feel very strong pride for a short time.

Buying a larger house also causes a large increase in rank, but not as suddenly. The probability of the purchase slowly approaches 100% over a few years. As the probability approaches 100%, so does the imagined rank of the homeowners. As their imagined rank continually increases over a few years, they continually feel weak pride.

Other Species

Rhesus monkeys feel pride. A study was conducted in which rhesus monkeys were paid cherry juice to view pictures of other monkeys. They were willing to be paid less juice to view higher-ranking monkeys. Viewing higher-ranking monkeys triggered their pride, just like being treated as an equal by a higher-ranking individual triggers pride in humans. The study, *Monkey Pay Per View: Adaptive Valuation of Social Images by Rhesus Macaques*, was conducted at Duke University by Robert Deaner.

CHAPTER 22

HUMILIATION

Type of Emotion:	conceptual punishment
Conceptual Trigger:	" my rank has decreased "
Mental Effect:	negative
Key Features:	the larger the decrease, the stronger the effect effect generally stronger in men
Involuntary Expression:	blushing, if humiliation stops pride
Synonyms:	embarrassment, shame, dejection

<u>Purpose</u>

Humiliation encourages everyone to maintain their rank.

Your rank falls when you are expected to contribute less to group happiness. The employed fail to maintain their rank when they become unemployed.

Contributing less to group happiness harms group survival. The more unemployed there are, the less efficient a nation is.

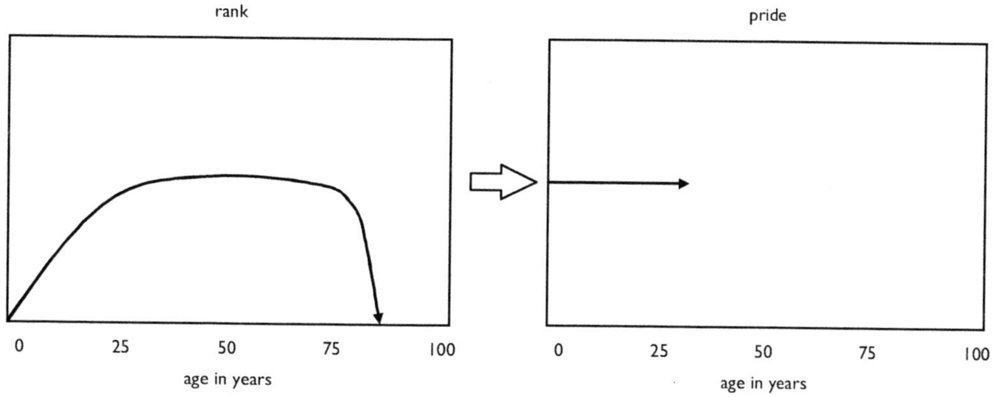

Rank is most likely to fall when rank plateaus and pride stops. Most people hit a rank plateau in their thirties. The continuous pride they felt throughout childhood stops. This is when people experience a mid-life crisis, meaning they think about letting their rank fall. Without the reward of pride, they are less willing to work long hours.

Humiliation maintains rank when pride stops. After hitting a plateau, people maintain their rank to avoid humiliation. They cannot imagine moving to a smaller house or wearing cheaper clothes. They decide that feeling humiliation is worse than working long hours without feeling pride. They give up on weekdays and live for weeknights, weekends and vacations.

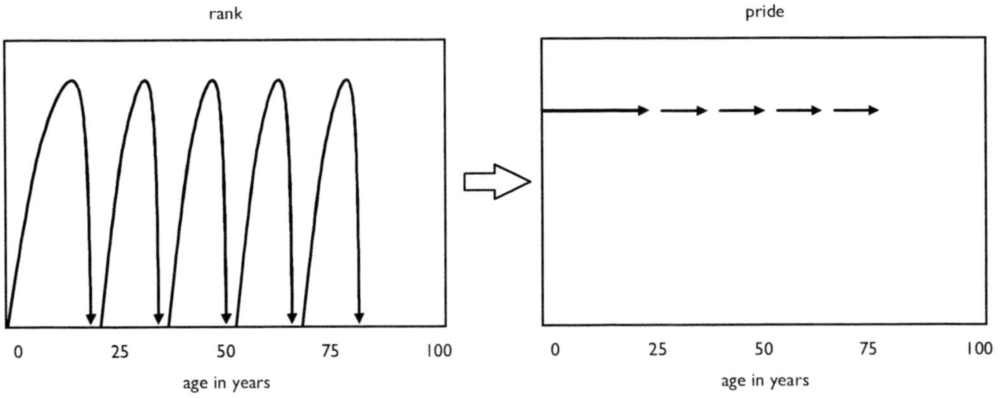

Without humiliation, people would roller-coaster on pride. Without a penalty to letting your rank fall, people would repeatedly let their rank drop to the bottom and then raise it back to its peak. Their nearly continuous increase in rank would trigger nearly continuous pride. CEO's would become alcoholics and then rise up to be CEO's again. Humiliation stops roller-coastering by penalizing the drops.

Rank also falls when innovation is not adopted. If you fail to adopt innovations like cell phones, your group contribution remains unchanged while others increase theirs.

Humiliation ensures the adoption of innovation. Most adults buying their first cell phone today are primarily doing so to avoid humiliation.

Conceptual Trigger

Humiliation is usually triggered when you:

- fail to graduate from school
- are fired, laid-off, demoted or retired
- are the favorite and you lose
- are the underdog and you lose by more than the spread
- are treated as an equal by a lower-ranking person
- are criticized or putdown
- are the victim of a prank
- apologize
- admit you are wrong or made a mistake
- do not hear others say please and thank-you when making a request
- ask for help, whether you are asking for directions or money
- learn that others have been allowed to break the rules with impunity

Humiliation is triggered by lower rank, not low rank. The only criminals who feel humiliation are first-time offenders. Every CEO feels humiliation when they retire.

	low rank	lower rank
top	✗	✓
nearly-top	✗	✓
above middle	✗	✓
middle	✗	✓
below middle	✗	✓
nearly-bottom	✓	✓
bottom	✗	✗

✗ not motivated

✓ motivated

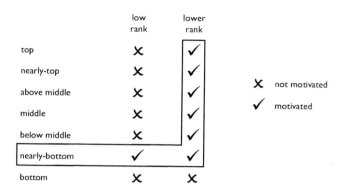

If humiliation was triggered by low rank, it would only motivate the nearly-bottom ranked. Those above the nearly-bottom ranked would not be motivated. They would not feel humiliation if their rank fell to the next level. The nearly-bottom ranked would be motivated. They would feel humiliation if their rank fell. The bottom rank would not be motivated to maintain their rank. They would still feel humiliation if they did.

Because humiliation is triggered by lower rank, it motivates everyone above the bottom rank. Everyone above the bottom rank feels humiliation when their rank falls. CEO's feel humiliation when they retire. Janitors feel humiliation when they lose their jobs.

By definition, humiliation is temporary. Humiliation is only triggered while you conclude that your rank is lower. Eventually, your lower rank is not lower anymore. A scratch on your car is embarrassing, but the embarrassment subsides after a few months.

Humiliation is triggered by slower growth. You will feel humiliation if you receive a 5% salary increase and others receive a 10% salary increase. This ensures that humiliation punishes those who are slow to adopt innovation.

Humiliation is not triggered by slower decline. You do not feel humiliation if you receive a 5% salary rollback and others receive a 10% salary rollback. This ensures that innovation during bad times is not punished. Instead, you are rewarded with pride.

Favorites always feel humiliation when they lose. Favorites are expected to win. Losing lowers their rank.

Favorites also feel humiliation if they win, but fail to beat the spread. Favorites are expected to win by the spread. Winning by less than the spread lowers their rank.

Underdogs only feel humiliation if they lose by more than the spread. Underdogs are expected to lose by the spread. Their rank only falls if they lose by more than the spread.

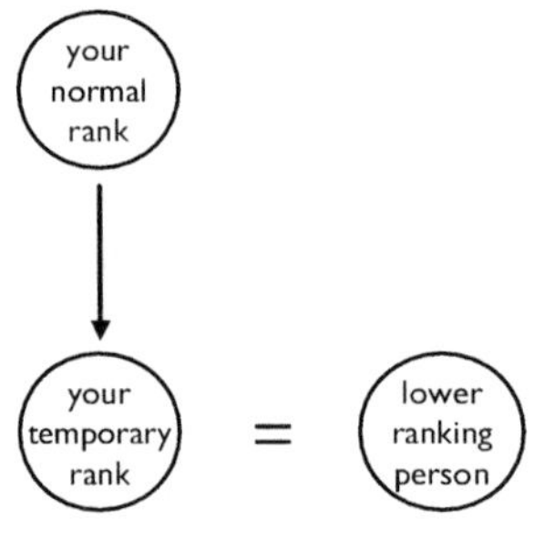

Being treated as an equal by a lower-ranking person triggers humiliation. If a lower-ranking person treats you like an equal, it feels like your rank has fallen to their level. Adults feel humiliation when a young child addresses them by their first name. The Queen feels humiliation when her subjects do not curtsey or bow for her.

Being criticized triggers humiliation. You feel humiliation when a superior tells you that you need to improve. You also feel humiliation when a friend tells you that you have bad breath.

Being putdown triggers humiliation. You feel humiliation the first few times someone says you are unattractive or unintelligent. Eventually, putdowns from that person do not decrease your rank further and therefore stop triggering humiliation.

Being the victim of a prank triggers humiliation. A prank cannot trigger humor in others unless it lowers someone's rank.

Apologizing triggers humiliation. If you apologize for being late, you are stating that your rank has fallen to that of somebody who is inconsiderate. People are reluctant to apologize because it triggers humiliation.

Admitting you are wrong or made a mistake triggers humiliation. You are acknowledging that you rank has fallen. People are reluctant to admit they are wrong because it triggers humiliation.

Not hearing others say please and thank-you triggers humiliation.

Saying please and thank-you is a promise of reciprocity. Saying "please pass the salt" is equivalent to saying "if you pass the salt, I will return the favor". Saying "thank you" is equivalent to saying "I confirm that I will return the favor".

If someone says please and thank-you to you, they are implying that you are equal-or-higher rank than they are. They do not expect you to cooperate with their request unless they promise reciprocity.

If someone does not say please and thank-you, they are implying that you are their servant. They expect you to cooperate with their request without a promise of reciprocity. If you thought you were equally-ranked, implying that you are a servant lowers your rank and triggers your humiliation.

We say please and thank-you to servants to mask the fact that they are lower rank. Customers and bosses say please and thank-you when dealing with waitresses or employees. They are polite to avoid triggering the servant's humiliation. Instead, they hope to trigger the servant's pride by treating them as an equal.

Asking for help triggers humiliation, whether you are asking for directions or money. Asking for help is often perceived as a signal of inferiority. Men do not like asking for directions because it signals a poor sense of orientation. Adults do not like asking for money because it signals inability to generate and manage money.

Allowing a few to break the rules with impunity triggers humiliation. If a few people are allowed to break the rules, it creates two ranks where there was one. Instead of one rank of rule abiders, there are now rule abiders and exceptions. The rule abiders are in a lower rank than before, which triggers their humiliation. People waiting in queues feel this humiliation when others are allowed to jump the queue.

Humiliation is triggered more frequently in an insecure person. Insecure people are frequently looking for evidence that others think they are lower rank. They frequently ask friends if their appearance or manner is embarrassing.

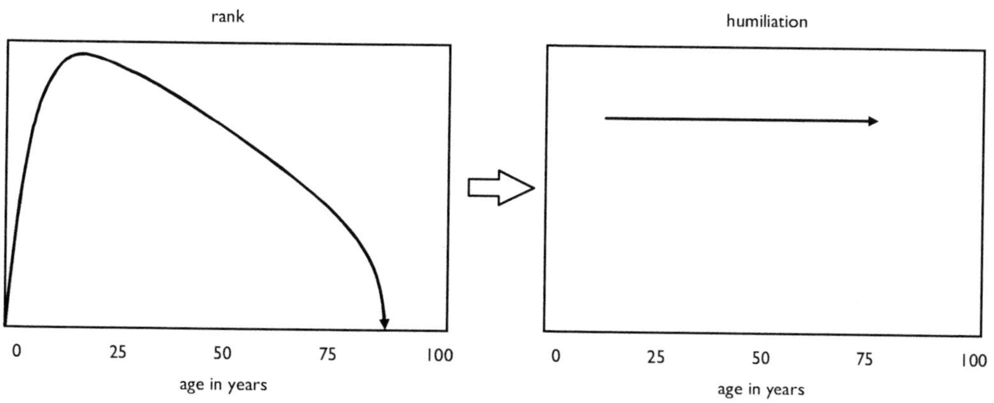

Child stars have the worst life plan. Child stars feel very strong pride as their rank rockets to the top. However, they usually spend the remainder of their lives continuously declining in rank. Their continuous decline in rank triggers continuous humiliation, which they often try to avoid with drugs or alcohol.

Mental Effect

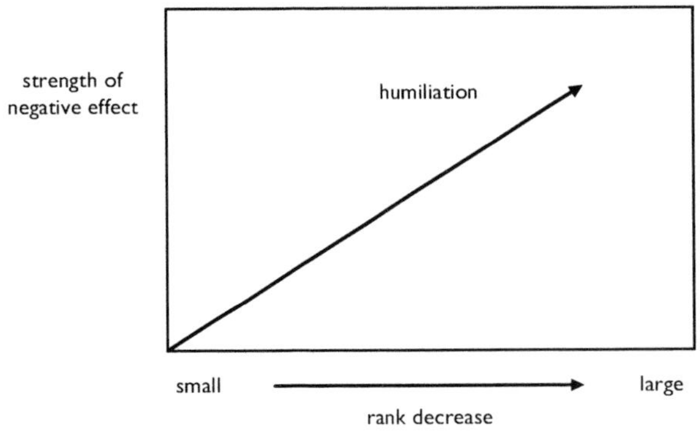

Humiliation varies with the rank decrease. The larger the decrease, the stronger the negative effect. Being fired triggers stronger humiliation than being criticized.

Humiliation varies with the rank decrease to mitigate losses to group happiness. To reduce the strength of humiliation, people will minimize their loss of rank. Professionals who lose their jobs will take a blue-collar job to avoid accepting welfare.

Humiliation is generally stronger in men. For the same decrease in rank, men feel a stronger negative effect than women. Men are more likely to commit suicide after losing a job or losing face.

The more public an apology, the stronger the humiliation. The more people know that you are a rule breaker, the further your rank falls. Successful libel plaintiffs often seek retribution by requesting a public apology from the defendant. The plaintiffs often request prominent placement of the apology in large daily newspapers to ensure maximum exposure.

High-ranking people face the greatest threat from humiliation. High-ranking people have the furthest to fall.

" The desire of acquiring the comforts of the world haunts the imagination of the poor, and the dread of losing them that of the rich. "

Alexis de Tocqueville

Pride and Humiliation

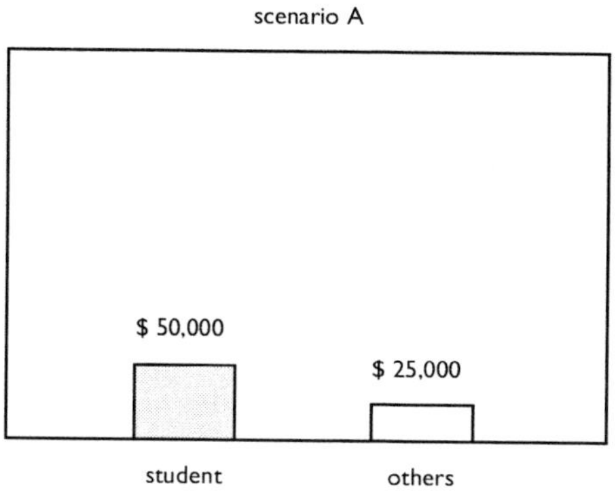

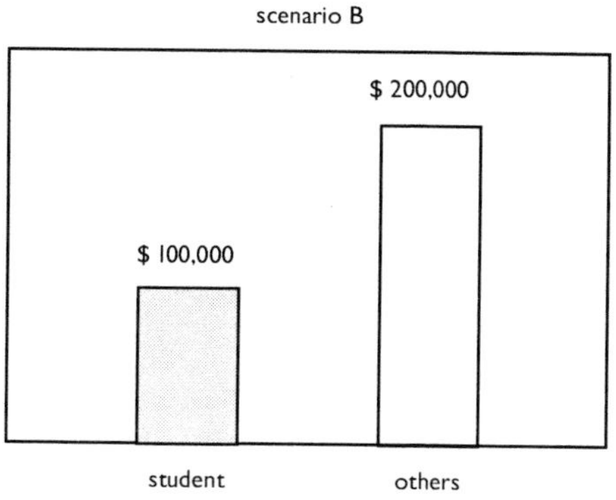

A survey of Harvard students compared humiliation and pride. Students were asked to choose scenario A or B. In scenario A, the student receives $50,000 and others receive $25,000. In scenario B, the student receives $100,000 and others receive $200,000.

Most students chose scenario A, even though it pays them half as much as B. Students preferred A because it triggered their pride, while B triggered their humiliation. The survey, *Is More Always Better?: A Survey on Positional Concerns (Journal of Economic Behavior and Organization)* was conducted by Sara Solnick And David Hemenway.

Other Species

Rhesus monkeys feel humiliation. In the *Monkey Pay Per View* study referred to in the previous chapter, monkeys had to be paid more cherry juice to view pictures of lower-ranking monkeys. Viewing lower-ranking monkeys triggered their humiliation, just like being treated as an equal by a lower-ranking individual triggers humiliation in humans.

Chapter 23

Humor

Type of Emotion:	conceptual reward
Conceptual Trigger:	" I learned that X made a rank-reducing mistake that I could have made "
Mental Effect:	positive
Key Features:	the more likely the mistake, the stronger the effect effect generally stronger in men
Voluntary Expression:	laughter
Synonyms:	funny, schadenfreude

Purpose

Humor encourages everyone to learn about rank-reducing mistakes that others make.

Learning about rank-reducing mistakes helps you avoid them. Learning about others becoming alcoholics makes you less likely to become an alcoholic.

Reducing rank-reducing mistakes helps group survival. The fewer alcoholics there are, the more efficient a nation is.

Conceptual Trigger

Humor is often triggered when you:

- hear a joke
- see a comedy
- hear a putdown
- witness a prank
- hear gossip
- read tabloid news
- see a favorite upset

Humor is triggered by lower rank, not low rank. Hearing about strangers begging is not enjoyable. Hearing about a former co-worker begging is.

Humor is triggered by mistakes, not misfortune. You feel humor when you see a man fall down because he stepped on a banana peel. You do not feel humor when you see a man fall down because of illness. Both men have dropped to the rank of people who cannot walk. However, the first man made the mistake of stepping on a banana peel and the second man had the misfortune of illness. You can learn from mistakes, you cannot learn from misfortune. Mistakes trigger humor. Misfortune triggers compassion.

Humor is only triggered by mistakes that you could make. Jokes about giving birth do not trigger humor in men. Jokes about erectile dysfunction do not trigger humor in women. Humor only rewards you for learning about mistakes that you could make.

Humor is only triggered the first time you learn about a mistake. Jokes are not funny the second time you hear them. Humor only rewards you for learning something new.

Humor is not triggered unless there is an unexpected reduction in rank. Watching or hearing an expected reduction of someone's rank does not trigger humor. If you expect someone's rank to be reduced, their rank is already lower in your mind. Clowns are not funny to adults. Adults know that clowns will reduce their rank.

Punch lines are funny because they provide an unexpected reduction in rank. ~ *Some sad news, President Bush's lapdog passed away. Gee, I didn't even know Tony Blair was sick.*

Putdowns and pranks trigger humor. If you witness a putdown or prank, you feel humor. If you are the target of a putdown or prank, you feel humiliation.

Self-effacing humor reduces the comedian's rank. The Three Stooges and Rodney Dangerfield were funny because they lowered their own rank. ~ *As a child, I got no respect. When I played in the sandbox, the cat kept covering me up.*

Witty jokes trigger humor and pride. Witty jokes also trigger pride because they require insight to be understood. Recognizing the insight elevates your rank to the comedian's rank. ~ *President Bush is waging war for the sake of the environment. He hopes to drive the price of oil so high that we stop driving cars.*

Witty putdowns also trigger humor and pride. ~ *You're a waste of carbon.*

Puns trigger pride, but not humor. Puns trigger pride because their play on words requires insight to identify. However, they do not lower someone's rank. ~ *I used to be a gold prospector, but it didn't pan out.*

Gossip triggers humor. Gossip is primarily about others losing rank. Friends talk about who is cheating on whom. Co-workers talk about who is being fired. Gossiping also triggers affection, which is true of any conversation.

Gossip triggers more humor than jokes or comedy. People spend a few hours a day conversing recreationally and gossip dominates those conversations. By comparison, people spend less than an hour a day listening to jokes or watching comedies.

Sports fans particularly enjoy upsets because they trigger pride and humor. By winning, the underdogs trigger their vicarious pride. By losing, the favorites trigger their humor.

Mental Effect

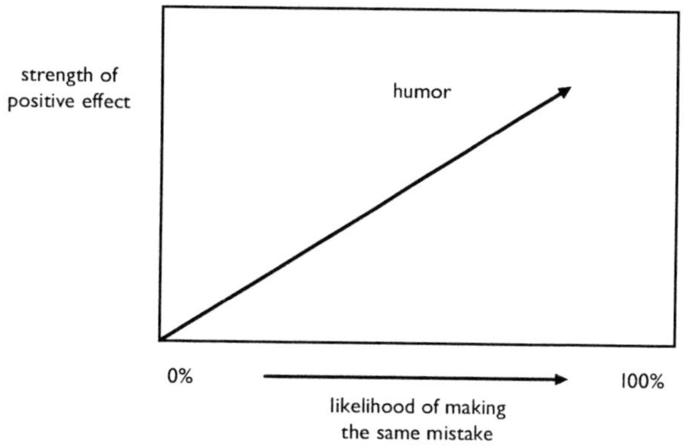

Humor varies with the likelihood of making the same mistake. The more likely it is that you could make the same mistake, the stronger the positive effect. Tabloid newspapers focus on famous actresses who are overweight or have a philandering husband because those are the mistakes tabloid readers are most likely to make.

Humor does not vary with the size of the other person's rank reduction. Unlike humiliation, humor is not stronger for larger rank reductions. You feel the same positive effect when another person's rank falls, regardless of how far it falls. You prefer gossiping about a neighbor to gossiping about a famous person. Although a famous person's rank can fall further, you are more likely to make the mistakes a neighbor makes. Tabloids focus on famous people because many readers know them, not because they have further to fall.

Humor is generally stronger in men. For mistakes that apply equally to both genders, men feel a stronger positive effect than women. Fraternity initiations humiliate pledges. Sorority initiations are friendly gatherings.

Humor seems stronger when it also stops envy. If you envy somebody, it is more enjoyable to see them make a rank-reducing mistake. Their mistake simultaneously triggers your humor and stops your envy. This is the tall-poppy syndrome. People prefer to criticize tall-poppies because it triggers humor and stops envy. The most vocal critics of tall-poppies are their former peers, who feel the strongest envy.

Humor seems stronger when it also stops revenge. If you hold a grudge against someone, it is more enjoyable to see them make a rank-reducing mistake. Their mistake simultaneously triggers your humor and stops your revenge. Spreading gossip about somebody is more enjoyable when the other person has spread gossip about you.

People joke about or criticize others for making mistakes they worry about making. The more somebody could make a particular rank-reducing mistake, the more they enjoy identifying others making that same mistake. People on diets are the first to joke about others being fat. People who have recently quit smoking are the most vocal critics of smoking.

Other Species

Chimpanzees feel humor.

" Georgia lives at the Yerkes National Primate Research Center in Atlanta, Georgia. When she sees visitors approaching, she hurries to the tap to collect a mouthful of water. She then mingles with the other chimps, and not even the best observer will spot anything unusual. Georgia can wait for minutes with closed lips until the visitors come near, then there are shrieks and laughs as she sprays them. "

Frans de Waal – *Suspicious Minds (NewScientist)*

CHAPTER 24

ENVY

Type of Emotion:	conceptual punishment
Conceptual Trigger:	" X, a former peer, is now higher rank than me "
Mental Effect:	negative
Key Features:	the more similar the peer, the stronger the effect effect generally stronger in men
Synonym:	not jealousy

Purpose

Envy encourages everyone to reach their highest potential rank.

Envy punishes you if a former peer achieves higher rank than you. You envy siblings and classmates who are paid more than you. You envy co-workers who are promoted ahead of you.

Higher-ranking former peers are good proxies for your highest potential rank. Siblings had the same genes and childhood experience. Classmates and co-workers had the same rank and opportunities.

Envy is stopped by matching a higher-ranking peer. You stop envying a wealthier sibling or classmate when you become equally wealthy. You stop envying a senior co-worker when you are promoted to their level.

Envy acts like a non-urgent coercion. Coercions are negative effects that stop if you take action. Revenge, for example, stops when you retaliate. Envy is also a negative effect that stops if you take action. Envy stops if you increase your rank to match a higher-ranking peer.

Striving to reach your highest potential rank helps group survival. The more everyone strives for their highest potential rank, the more efficient a nation is.

Conceptual Trigger

Envy is often triggered when:

- a sibling receives more parental attention
- a competitor wins an award and you do not
- a college classmate buys a bigger house than you
- a co-worker is given a larger office than you
- a neighbor buys a better car than you
- you attend a school reunion

Envy is triggered by higher rank, not high rank. You do not envy a stranger driving a much better car than yours, like a Rolls Royce or a Ferrari. You do envy a sibling who drives a slightly better car than you.

Envy is only triggered by former peers. You envy a co-worker who is promoted ahead of you. You do not envy employees who are promoted at levels above or below you.

Reunions intensively trigger all four rank emotions. Reunions put many peers together to discuss how their ranks have changed. Pride, humiliation, humor and envy are being continuously triggered and the mental effects are strong.

Mental Effect

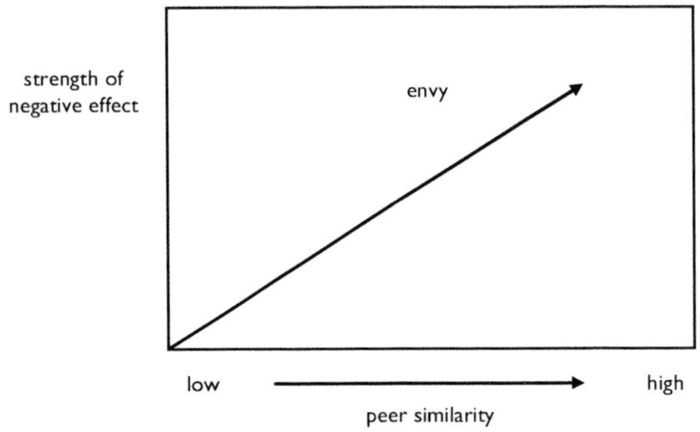

Envy varies with peer similarity. The more similar a peer's circumstances, the stronger the negative effect. Siblings usually trigger the strongest envy because they usually have the most similar circumstances.

Envy does not vary with the size of the peer's rank increase. Unlike pride, envy is not stronger for larger increases in rank. You feel the same envy towards two brothers if one buys a house twice the size of yours and the other buys a house ten times the size of yours.

Envy is generally stronger in men. For the same peer similarity, men feel a stronger negative effect than women. Men are more concerned about differences in wealth. Men are more concerned about co-workers being promoted ahead of them.

Unlike the other rank emotions, envy is permanent. The other rank emotions stop without any effort on your part. Pride stops when your higher rank is not higher anymore. Humiliation stops when your lower rank is not lower anymore. Humor stops the second time you learn about another's mistake. Envy does not stop unless you close the gap between you and your higher-ranking former peer.

The best reason to be top ranked is not feeling envy. The pride you feel is temporary. The envy that your former peers feel is permanent, unless they increase their rank.

Other Species

Capuchin monkeys feel envy. Capuchin monkeys will take grapes or cucumber if offered, but prefer grapes. They will take cucumber if they see that another monkey is given cucumber. They will not take cucumber if they see that another monkey is given grapes. *Monkeys Reject Unequal Pay (Nature)* summarizes this research, which was led by Sarah Brosnan and Frans de Waal.

Chimpanzees feel envy and revenge. In California, captive chimpanzees attacked a man who was giving another chimp special treatment. The attacking chimpanzees bit off the man's nose, foot and testicles. They attacked when they saw the man bring a birthday cake to another chimp. The man had been making daily visits to the birthday chimp during the eight weeks preceding the attack. This visit was different because it included a cake. *Birthday Party Turns Bloody When Chimps Attack* was reported by *USA Today*.

Chapter 25

Sensations

emotions

	conceptions	sensations	reflexes	involuntary expressions	voluntary expressions
individual		pleasing taste, hunger, disgust	startle fear		
genetic	maternal love & grief grandmaternal love & grief monogynistic love & grief infatuation, heartbreak jealousy, adulterous guilt	sexual pleasure, lust, repugnance affection, cute, loneliness		horror momentary frowning prolonged frowning momentary smiling crying	
group	revenge, criminal guilt compassion, selfish guilt pride, humiliation humor, envy	excitement, boredom		prolonged smiling blushing	anger laughter
purpose	direct your behavior	direct your behavior	help you avoid threats	direct behavior of others	direct behavior of others
trigger	conclusions	sensory stimuli	conclusions or sensory stimuli	conception, sensation or reflex	habitual decision
mental effects	positive or negative	positive or negative	suppressive	none	none
physical effects	none	almost none	defensive	facial expressions	facial & vocal expressions

	rewards	coercions	punishments
survival	pleasing taste	hunger	disgust
sexual	sexual pleasure	lust	repugnance
social	affection, cute	loneliness	
scenic	excitement	boredom	

There are three types of sensation: rewards, coercions and punishments.

Rewards are positive effects triggered by the presence of sensory stimuli. Pleasing taste is triggered by the taste of food.

Coercions are negative effects triggered by the absence of sensory stimuli and stopped by its return. Hunger is triggered by the absence of food and stopped by its return.

Punishments are negative effects triggered by the presence of sensory stimuli. Disgust is triggered by the smell of animal toxins, like fecal matter.

Non-sexual sensations can be triggered at birth or within a few months of birth. Sexual sensations cannot be triggered until puberty. Cute cannot be triggered until 33 months.

Sensations fall into four categories of purpose: survival, sexual, social and scenic.

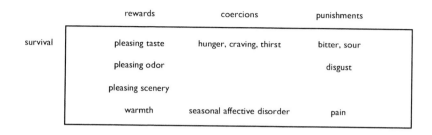

	rewards	coercions	punishments
survival	pleasing taste	hunger, craving, thirst	bitter, sour
	pleasing odor		disgust
	pleasing scenery		
	warmth	seasonal affective disorder	pain

There are many survival sensations. Survival rewards include pleasing taste, pleasing odor, pleasing scenery and warmth. Survival coercions include hunger, craving, thirst and seasonal affective disorder (SAD). Survival punishments include bitter, sour, disgust and pain.

Survival sensations encourage eating and avoiding physical harm. Survival rewards reward you for eating. Survival coercions coerce you to eat. Survival punishments punish you for detecting toxins or suffering trauma.

Eating and avoiding physical harm are the only behaviors that help your survival. All other behaviors harm your survival to help your genes or your group.

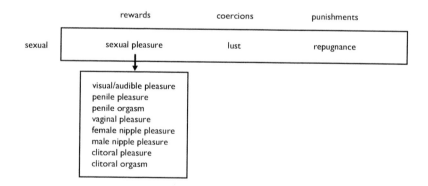

	rewards	coercions	punishments
sexual	sexual pleasure	lust	repugnance

sexual pleasure ↓

- visual/audible pleasure
- penile pleasure
- penile orgasm
- vaginal pleasure
- female nipple pleasure
- male nipple pleasure
- clitoral pleasure
- clitoral orgasm

Sexual pleasure consists of eight different sensory rewards: visual/audible pleasure, penile pleasure, penile orgasm, vaginal pleasure, female nipple pleasure, male nipple pleasure, clitoral pleasure and clitoral orgasm.

Most sexual sensations encourage mating. Sexual pleasure primarily rewards men for mating. Lust coerces men if they do not. Repugnance punishes men for courting kin.

	rewards	coercions	punishments
social	affection, cute	loneliness	

Social sensations encourage kin interaction. Affection and cute reward you for interacting with kin. Loneliness coerces you if you do not. Kin interaction transfers knowledge to future generations.

	rewards	coercions	punishments
scenic	excitement	boredom	

Scenic sensations encourage exploring for new scenery. Excitement rewards you for finding new scenery. Boredom coerces you if you do not. Exploring for new scenery helps groups expand their territory.

CHAPTER 26

SURVIVAL REWARDS

Specific Sensations:	pleasing taste, pleasing odor, pleasing scenery, warmth
Sensory Trigger:	food or the places where food is found
Mental Effect:	positive
Key Features:	the more concentrated the stimuli, the stronger the effect effect fades with repeated short-term exposure
Physical Effect:	salivation

Purpose

Survival rewards encourage everyone to eat and live near food.

Sensory Triggers

Pleasing taste is triggered by the taste of food. Four pleasing tastes have been identified so far: sweet, salty, fatty and umami. Sweet is triggered by fruit. Salty is triggered by salt and marine seafood. Fatty taste is triggered by food with lipids, like hamburgers and fries. Umami or savory taste is triggered by foods with free glutamates, like parmesan cheese or tomatoes. Umami is more pleasing when combined with salt, which makes ketchup and soy sauce popular condiments.

Pleasing odor is triggered by the smell of food. Flavor is the combination of pleasing taste and pleasing odor which is triggered as food travels over your tongue and releases odors upwards into your nasal cavity. There are numerous pleasing flavors because there are numerous pleasing odors, not because there are numerous tastes. The importance of odor can be noticed during a cold. Food has little flavor when your nose is congested.

Pleasing odor can also be triggered by the smell of places where food is found. We enjoy perfumes because they smell like flowers. Flowers grow where fruit is found.

Pleasing scenery is triggered by the sight of places where food is found. We pay premiums for real estate that faces water and green spaces. We put windows in our walls to see outside vegetation. If we cannot see outside vegetation, we bring vegetation inside or hang landscape paintings on the walls.

Warmth is triggered by sunlight. Sunlight enables your skin to produce vitamin D, another type of food you need to consume. People enjoy warmth when they sunbathe.

Warmth and warming up are different. Warming up feels good because it stops cold, a type of pain.

Water and oxygen do not trigger a pleasing taste or pleasing odor. Water is not food. Oxygen is food, but is consumed involuntarily.

Mental Effect

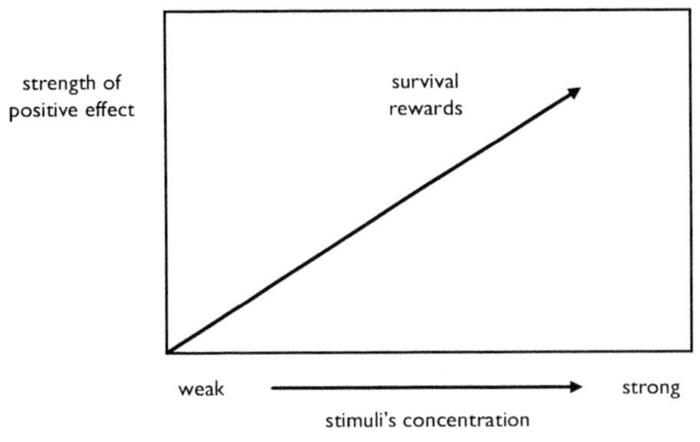

Survival rewards vary with a stimuli's concentration. The higher the concentration, the stronger the positive effect. The higher a food's sugar content, the more pleasing it tastes. The more lush the scenery, the more pleasing it appears.

Survival rewards fade with repeated short-term exposure. The first taste of food triggers the strongest effect. The second taste triggers a weaker effect than the first and so on. This short-term fading discourages eating too much.

Modern Eating

Increased flavor variety has contributed to overeating.

In the past, we only ate a few flavors. After a few mouthfuls, meals were not pleasing. We kept eating to avoid hunger, not to enjoy pleasing taste.

Today's greatly expanded variety of flavors makes meals enjoyable from start to finish. As soon as one flavor stops triggering pleasing taste, we switch to a new flavor. After the appetizer and main course, everyone always has room for dessert.

We exercise more than necessary so we can eat more than necessary. To enjoy survival rewards as much as possible, we exercise to burn off the extra calories we eat but do not need. While we can burn off extra calories, our bodies are not built for the overuse, as evidenced by the growing numbers of hip replacements.

Chapter 27

Survival Coercions

Specific Sensations:	hunger, craving, thirst, seasonal affective disorder (SAD)
Sensory Triggers:	absence of food or water
Mental Effect:	negative
Sensory Stops:	food or water
Key Feature:	effect grows stronger with time

Purpose

Survival coercions encourage everyone to avoid malnutrition and dehydration.

Coercions add to your motivation, but only when necessary. Pleasing taste always encourages you to eat. Hunger also encourages you to eat, but only when you have not eaten recently. The alternative to temporary hunger is permanently stronger pleasing taste, which would cause too much eating. Eating would always be better than sex.

Sensory Triggers

Hunger is triggered when you need food.

Cravings are triggered when you need a particular nutrient. In war-torn Germany, pregnant women craved plaster. Their unborn children were depleting their calcium levels. Milk, their main source of calcium, was scarce. Plaster, which contains calcium, was abundant thanks to the Allied bombing of civilians.

Thirst is triggered when you need water. You become thirsty when you do not consume enough water with your food.

Seasonal Affective Disorder (SAD) is triggered when you need vitamin D. SAD is most prevalent in northern latitudes during March, when the sun's rays have been oblique for a few months. Canadians refer to this feeling as cabin fever.

Mental Effect

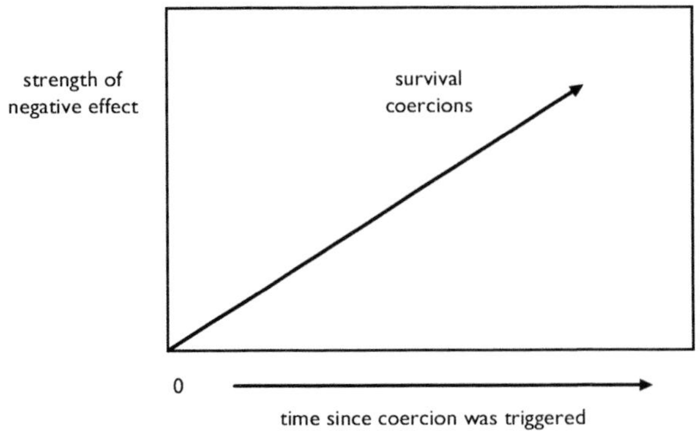

Survival coercions vary with time. The longer a coercion has been triggered, the stronger the negative effect. The longer you have been hungry, the stronger your hunger feels.

Survival coercions grow stronger as necessary to ensure eating or drinking. As your hunger or thirst grows stronger, you are more motivated to overcome obstacles to eating or drinking.

Sensory Stops

Survival coercions are stopped by consuming food or water. Hunger is stopped by eating food. Cravings are stopped by eating a particular nutrient. Thirst is stopped by drinking water. SAD is stopped by going outside on a sunny day.

Chapter 28

Survival Punishments

Specific Sensations:	bitter, sour, disgust, pain
Sensory Triggers:	toxins or trauma
Mental Effect:	negative
Key Features:	the more concentrated the stimuli, the stronger the effect effect fades with repeated short-term exposure
Involuntary Expression:	momentary frowning
Physical Effect:	vomiting

Purpose

Survival punishments encourage everyone to avoid toxins and trauma.

Sensory Triggers

Bitter and sour are triggered by plant toxins. Most poisonous plants are bitter. Most rotting plants are sour.

Disgust is triggered by animal toxins. Disgust is triggered by feces, urine, vomit or rotting flesh. Disgust is not triggered by a person's behavior.

Pain is triggered by physical trauma.

Mental Effect

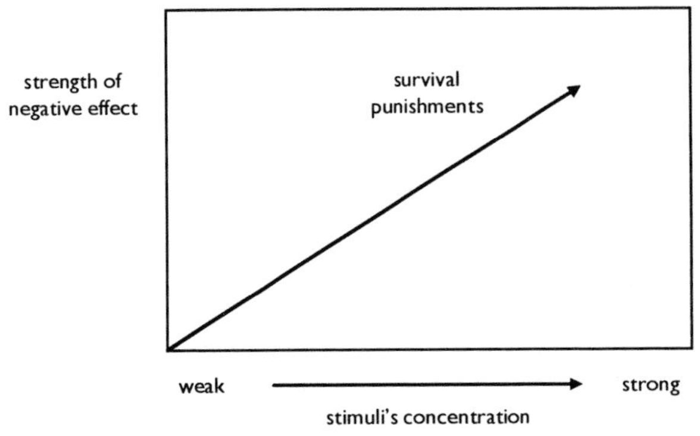

Survival punishments vary with a stimuli's concentration. The higher the stimuli's concentration, the stronger the negative effect. The closer you are to fecal matter, the more disgusting it smells.

Survival punishments fade with repeated short-term exposure. Farmers working with manure do not notice its odor by the end of the day. This short-term fading helps you. If you cannot avoid a toxin or trauma, it does not help to continue punishing you.

Chapter 29

Visual / Audible Pleasure

Type of Emotion:	sensory reward
Sensory Triggers:	the visual and audible differences that separate pre-menopausal, non-pregnant women from other humans
Mental Effect:	positive
Key Features:	the more incorrect humans excluded, the stronger the effect the closer to the reproductive ideal, the stronger the effect the more novelty, the stronger the effect
Physical Effect:	penile erection

Purpose

Visual/audible pleasure encourages men to court women.

Female visual/audible pleasure did not evolve. Female visual/audible pleasure did not evolve because male visual/audible pleasure did. Only one gender needs to travel to the other for mating to occur.

This gender difference can be seen in pornography sales and clothing choices.

Women buy a tiny percentage of the pornography sold. Men buy virtually all of the pornographic movies and magazines. Men are virtually all of the customers for telephone sex. Men are virtually all of the customers in strip clubs. If women do visit a strip club, they go with a group of friends as a novel way to socialize.

Men do not dress to be sexually appealing, but women do. Women wear bras, high heels, plunging necklines, skirts, pantyhose and thongs to trigger visual pleasure in men. Men do not make themselves similarly uncomfortable to be visually appealing to women.

Women can feel infatuation or sexual pleasure when looking at a man. These positive effects are mistakenly believed to be female visual pleasure.

Infatuation is triggered when a woman sees a man looking at her. If a woman sees a man looking at her, she can conclude that she triggers his visual pleasure.

Infatuation is also triggered when a woman sees an erect penis. If a woman sees that a man has an erection while looking at her, she can confidently conclude that she triggers his visual pleasure.

Sexual pleasure can be triggered by imagining sex. Women enjoy looking at a man's bum because they imagine it thrusting, which helps them imagine vaginal pleasure.

Sensory Triggers

Visual pleasure is triggered by the sight of:

- protruding breasts
- plump lips
- wide hips
- slender appendages - head, face, neck, arms, hands, legs, feet
- 8% shorter height
- beardless face
- pubic hair
- non-grey hair
- narrow waist

Audible pleasure is triggered by the sound of an adult female voice talking, laughing, singing or moaning.

Visual pleasure is not triggered by female genitalia. Female genitalia was not visible before Brazilian waxing.

Visual pleasure is not triggered by eyes. Eyes are not a feature that separates women from other humans. Women apply make-up in the mistaken belief that eyes trigger visual pleasure.

Eyes do trigger affection. Affection is triggered by differences between humans and other primates, such as the unique white sclera of human eyes. Women feel the affection that white eyes trigger when they are looking in the mirror while applying make-up. Eye make-up amplifies affection, not visual pleasure.

Mental Effect

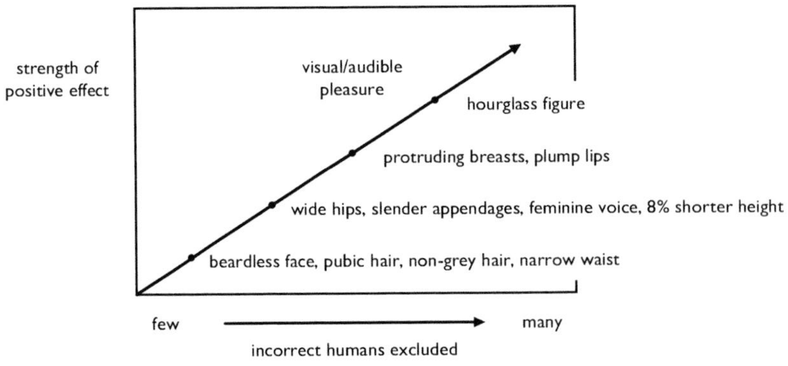

Visual/audible pleasure varies with the incorrect humans excluded. The more incorrect humans are excluded by a feature, the stronger the positive effect.

	types of humans excluded					correct humans
	men	children	post menopausal women	visibly pregnant women	not-visibly pregnant women	pre-menopausal non-pregnant women
hourglass figure	X	X	X	X		
protruding breasts	X	X	X			
plump lips	X	X	X			
wide hips	X	X				
slender appendages	X	X				
feminine voice	X	X				
8% shorter height	X	X				
beardless face	X					
pubic hair		X				
non-grey hair			X			
narrow waist				X		

Incorrect humans are men, children, post-menopausal women, visibly pregnant women and not-visibly pregnant women. Correct humans are pre-menopausal, non-pregnant women.

An hourglass figure excludes the most incorrect humans. An hourglass figure is the combination of three features: protruding breasts, a narrow waist and wide hips. The only incorrect humans not excluded by this combination are not-visibly pregnant women.

Protruding breasts and plump lips exclude men, children and post-menopausal women.

Wide hips, slender appendages, feminine voice and 8% shorter height exclude men and children.

Beardless face, pubic hair, non-grey hair and narrow waist exclude one category each. Beardless face excludes men. Pubic hair excludes children. Non-grey hair excludes post-menopausal women. Narrow waist excludes visibly pregnant women.

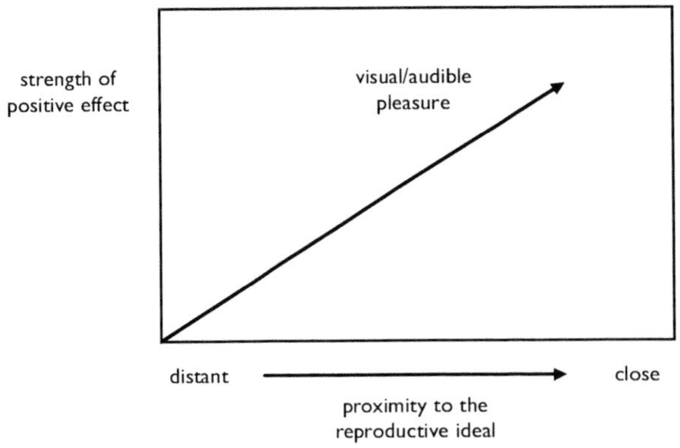

Visual/audible pleasure also varies with a feature's proximity to the reproductive ideal. The closer an individual feature is to the ideal, the stronger the positive effect. The reproductive ideal is what best helps a woman to conceive, gestate, give birth to, breastfeed and protect a child.

Ideal breasts are large and do not sag. Breasts have an optimal size. Freakishly large breasts trigger weaker visual pleasure than average breasts. Sagging influences visual pleasure more than size. Small, non-sagging breasts trigger stronger visual pleasure than large, sagging breasts. Sagging indicates post-menopausal.

Ideal lips are more plump than men's and children's. Like breasts, lips have an optimal size. Freakishly large lips trigger weaker visual pleasure than average lips.

The ideal waist-to-hip ratio is 0.7. Women without narrow waists may be pregnant. Women without wide hips may be sexually immature. The waist-to-hip ratio is explored indepth by Devendra Singh in *Adaptive Significance of Female Physical Attractiveness: Role of Waist-to-Hip Ratio (Journal of Personality and Social Psychology).*

Ideal appendages are not muscular, chubby or thin. Muscularity indicates masculinity. Chubbiness indicates sexual immaturity. Thinness indicates illness or malnourishment.

Ideal voice has a pitch and resonance midway between men and children.

Ideal height for a woman is 8% shorter than a man, which is approximately 6 inches. More than 6 inches shorter indicates sexual immaturity. Less than 6 inches shorter indicates masculinity. Average women are more attractive than tiny or tall women.

Ideal face is hairless, symmetrical, blemish-free and taut. Bearded faces indicate masculinity. Asymmetric faces indicate genetic defects. Blemished faces indicate illness. Sagging faces indicate post-menopausal.

Ideal hair is shiny, thick and not grey. Dull or thin hair indicates illness or malnourishment. Grey hair indicates post-menopausal.

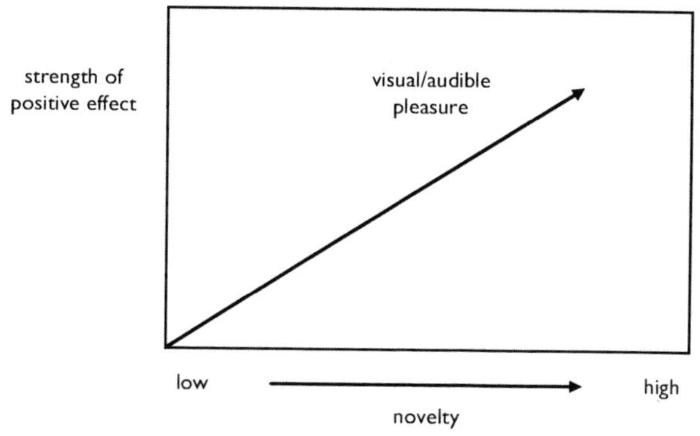

Visual/audible pleasure also varies with a woman's novelty. The more novel a woman appears or sounds to a man, the stronger the positive effect. Women frequently change their appearance to maximize their novelty. Women often seem more attractive to men when they have a foreign accent.

Men preferred blondes because they were novel. Thanks to hair coloring, blonde hair has lost its novelty. Consequently, more women are dying their hair red to be novel.

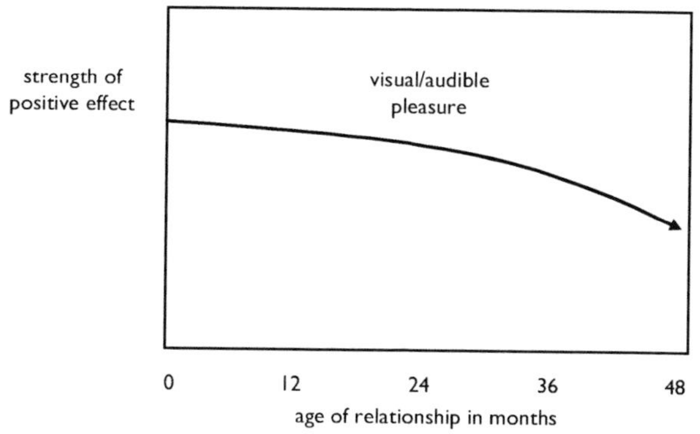

Women become less attractive to men. As a woman becomes less novel to a man, she triggers weaker visual/audible pleasure. Even the most beautiful women become increasingly less attractive to a man. The husbands of supermodels cheat on their wives as much as other men do.

Both sexes become less attractive to each other. Shortly after the start of courtship, a woman begins triggering increasingly weaker visual/audible pleasure in a man. After 8 months of courtship, a man no longer triggers infatuation in a woman.

The preference for novelty encourages men to prefer new women, which increases the genetic diversity of their offspring.

Beards

Beards evolved to stop men courting men. Beards evolved during our aquatic detour, when our heads were the only body part routinely visible above water. *The Aquatic Ape Hypothesis*, by Elaine Morgan, explores our aquatic detour indepth.

Erect Penis

Visual pleasure is also triggered by the sight of an erect penis. Men feel visual pleasure when they see another man's erect penis.

Men prefer pornography that shows an erect penis. The vast majority of heterosexual pornographic movies include men with erect penises, not just naked women. The most important scenes are the cum shots which feature a close-up of an erect penis.

The triggering of visual pleasure by the sight of an erect penis would have been helpful during multi-male mating. Multi-male mating is multiple males mating with the same female within hours of each other. Males in primate species that use multi-male mating also feel visual pleasure when they see an erect penis. It causes them to develop an erection, which prepares them to mate when the opportunity arises.

The triggering of visual pleasure by the sight of an erect penis has probably led men to mistakenly believe they are homosexual.

CHAPTER 30

PENILE PLEASURE

Type of Emotion:	sensory reward
Sensory Trigger:	copulation or contact that replicates it
Mental Effect:	positive
Key Features:	effect grows stronger with sustained copulation minimum duration of 120 seconds to reach orgasm threshold
Physical Effect:	penile erection

<u>Purpose</u>

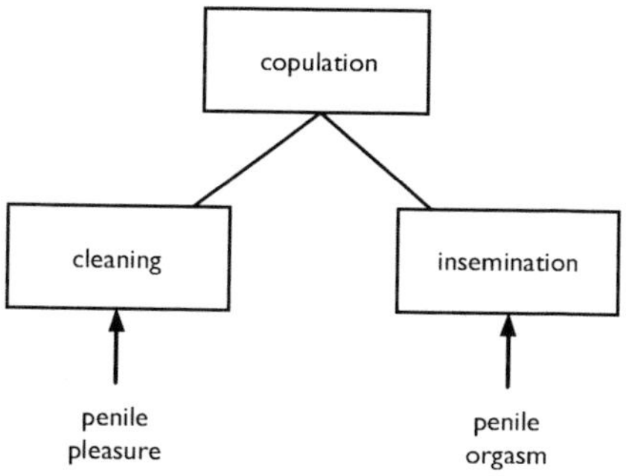

Penile pleasure encourages men to clean women.

Copulation is cleaning followed by insemination. Cleaning has a minimum duration of 120 seconds to reach the orgasm threshold. Insemination has a fixed duration of 6 seconds. Cleaning is encouraged by penile pleasure. Insemination is encouraged by penile orgasm.

Cleaning is not required for insemination. Cleaning is not the norm. Males in many species only require one or two thrusts to complete insemination.

Cleaning is common in species using multi-male mating, like chimpanzees. Cleaning removes seminal deposits from previous males.

Multi-male mating does not explain extended human cleaning. Chimpanzees only clean for 10 seconds, despite using multi-male mating far more than humans do and they have the testicles to prove it. Relative to their body weight, chimpanzee testicles are 4 times heavier than human testicles.

Our aquatic detour explains our extended cleaning. During our aquatic detour, we lived and mated in the water. Cleaning would have removed marine deposits already present in the vagina or pushed into the vagina during initial penetration.

The baculum and hymen are further reproductive evidence of our aquatic detour. Among our closest primate relatives, only humans are missing a baculum and only humans have a hymen. Human males lost their baculum, which is a penis bone, because waves broke it during mating. Human females gained a hymen to prevent marine pathogens from entering the vagina during childhood.

The penis is shaped to help with cleaning and insemination. The bulbous head of the penis acts like a bi-directional flange as it rides over deposits during vaginal penetration and then bends back to scoop deposits out when the penis withdraws. When the head is fully erect, as it is during orgasm, it pushes deposits forward and scoops nothing out when it withdraws. Most primates, including chimpanzees, did not evolve a bulbous head or true glans penis.

Sensory Trigger

Penile pleasure is triggered by copulation or contact that replicates it.

Masturbation replicates copulation. Masturbation is more common in humans than other species. Appendages that are good for using tools are also good for replicating copulation. Masturbation is less common in horses and bears.

Mental Effect

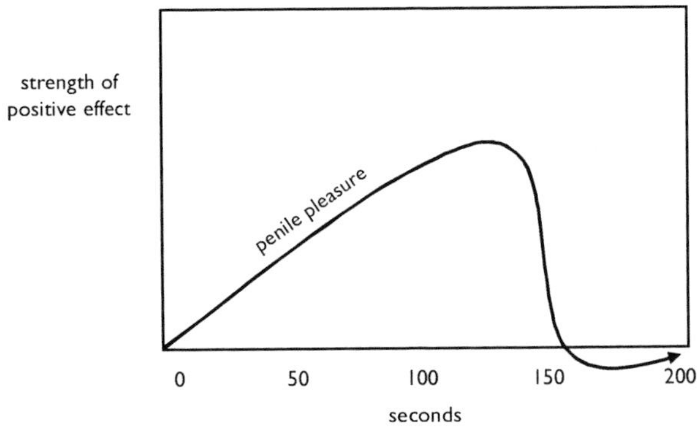

Penile pleasure grows stronger with sustained copulation or cleaning. This encourages men to penetrate and withdraw once a second for a minimum of 120 seconds. This frequency and duration ensures the removal of pre-existing vaginal deposits.

After penile orgasm, penile pleasure temporarily becomes a weak negative effect. This discourages men from cleaning their own seminal deposit.

Chapter 31

Penile Orgasm

Type of Emotion: sensory reward

Sensory Trigger: total pleasure threshold is reached

Mental Effect: positive

Key Feature: fixed duration of 6 seconds

Physical Effects: ejaculation, erection termination, lethargy

Purpose

Penile orgasm encourages men to inseminate women.

Penile orgasm also encourages men to court and clean women. Penile orgasm adds to the motivation to court and clean already provided by visual/audible and penile pleasure. While they act like a salary, penile orgasm acts like a bonus payment. Visual/audible and penile pleasure reward men with moderately strong pleasure as they court and clean. Penile orgasm rewards men with very strong pleasure, but only if they successfully complete courting and cleaning.

Sensory Trigger

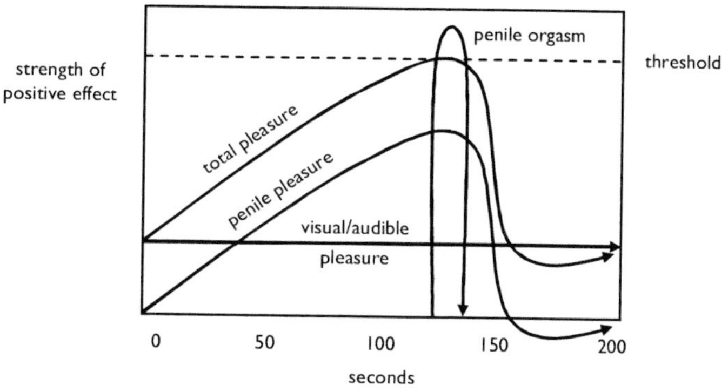

Penile orgasm is triggered when total pleasure reaches a threshold. Total pleasure is the combined strength of penile pleasure and visual/audible pleasure.

Reaching the threshold requires strong penile pleasure. Strong penile pleasure requires at least 120 seconds of cleaning before insemination.

Reaching the threshold also requires strong visual/audible pleasure. Simply put, men cannot reach orgasm without seeing, hearing or imagining a woman. This requirement encourages men to reach orgasm with women.

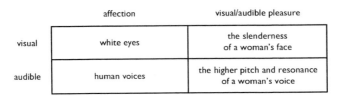

	affection	visual/audible pleasure
visual	white eyes	the slenderness of a woman's face
audible	human voices	the higher pitch and resonance of a woman's voice

Affection may also help men reach the total pleasure threshold. It seems to be easier for men to reach orgasm when a woman makes eye contact or talks to them. If affection helps men reach the orgasm threshold, it would encourage men to reach orgasm with women.

Separating the role of affection and visual/audible pleasure is difficult because they are triggered by the same features or neighboring features. Visual affection is triggered by white eyes. Visual pleasure is triggered by the slenderness of a woman's face. Audible affection is triggered by human voices. Audible pleasure is triggered by the slightly higher pitch and resonance of a woman's voice.

Mental Effect

Unlike other sensory rewards, the strength and duration of orgasm does not vary. It is always a very strong positive effect with a duration of 6 seconds.

Erectile dysfunction drugs do not affect the strength of penile pleasure or penile orgasm. Viagra, Cialis and Levitra only affect penile erection. They do not improve sexual pleasure for men with normal erectile function.

Physical Effect

Penile orgasm triggers ejaculation.

Penile orgasm also terminates penile erection. Men cannot achieve an erection for a few hours after orgasm. This prevents men from cleaning their own deposits.

Penile orgasm also induces lethargy. By staying with a woman, a lethargic man discourages other men from attempting to mate with her and clean his deposit.

Chapter 32

Vaginal Pleasure

Type of Emotion:	sensory reward
Sensory Trigger:	copulation or contact that replicates it
Mental Effect:	positive
Key Feature:	effect elevated during infatuation's 4 month plateau
Physical Effect:	vaginal lubrication when elevated

Purpose

Vaginal pleasure encourages women to tolerate copulation.

Sensory Trigger

Vaginal pleasure is triggered by copulation or contact that replicates it.

Mental Effect

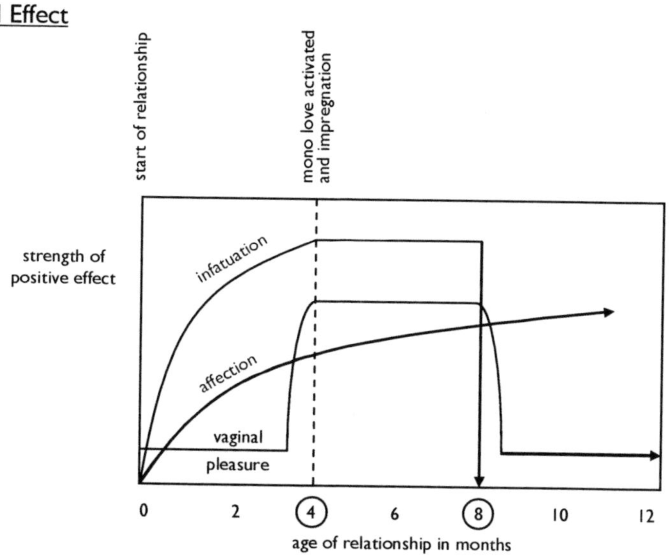

Vaginal pleasure is elevated during infatuation's 4 month plateau. If women feel strong infatuation and affection, they must have activated a man's monogynistic love. With the guarantee of 42 months of male support, women are encouraged to mate by an elevation in vaginal pleasure. During these 4 months, women almost enjoy sex as much as men do.

Unlike penile pleasure, vaginal pleasure does not grow stronger with sustained copulation.

Chapter 33

Vaginal Orgasm

Vaginal orgasm did not evolve.

Vaginal orgasm is not required. Copulation requires almost no voluntary behavior from women. They just need to tolerate it.

Women do experience clitoral orgasm. Clitoral orgasm is a similarly strong positive effect mistakenly believed to be vaginal orgasm. Clitoral orgasm can be triggered by intercourse, but only if a man's pubic bone makes contact with a woman's clitoris. Vaginal pleasure can also help women reach the clitoral orgasm threshold.

The Case of the Female Orgasm, by Elisabeth Lloyd, provides an indepth exploration of the female orgasm in humans.

Other Species

Other primates have the same experience as human females: females do not reach orgasm during vaginal stimulation, but do reach orgasm during clitoral stimulation. *Primate Sexuality: Comparative Studies of the Prosimians, Monkeys, Apes and Human Beings* by Alan Dixson reviews the literature on female orgasm in primates.

CHAPTER 34

FEMALE NIPPLE PLEASURE

Type of Emotion:	sensory reward
Sensory Trigger:	breastfeeding or contact that replicates it
Mental Effect:	positive
Physical Effect:	nipple erection

Purpose

Female nipple pleasure encourages women to tolerate breastfeeding.

Chapter 35

Male Nipple Pleasure

Type of Emotion:	sensory reward
Sensory Trigger:	contact that replicates breastfeeding
Mental Effect:	positive
Key Feature:	functions like female nipple pleasure, but weaker effect
Physical Effect:	nipple erection

Purpose

Male nipple pleasure serves no purpose.

men	women
male nipples	female nipples
penis	clitoris

Male nipples are embryonic leftovers. Nerve endings that reach the epidermal envelope must be hardwired before an embryo's gender is set. Consequently, both genders have nipples and penises. Men have nipples where women have nipples. Men have a penis where women have a clitoris.

men	women
male nipple pleasure	female nipple pleasure
penile pleasure & orgasm	clitoral pleasure & orgasm

Male nipple pleasure is also an embryonic leftover. Embryonic hardwiring extends from the epidermal envelope to the positive effects triggered in the brain. Clitoral pleasure and clitoral orgasm are also embryonic leftovers.

CHAPTER 36

CLITORAL PLEASURE

Type of Emotion:	sensory reward
Sensory Trigger:	contact that replicates copulation
Mental Effect:	positive
Key Feature:	functions like penile pleasure, but weaker effect
Physical Effect:	clitoral erection

<u>Purpose</u>

Clitoral pleasure serves no purpose. The clitoris and clitoral pleasure are both embryonic leftovers.

<u>Sensory Trigger</u>

Clitoral pleasure is triggered by contact that replicates penile penetration of a vagina.

<u>Mental Effect</u>

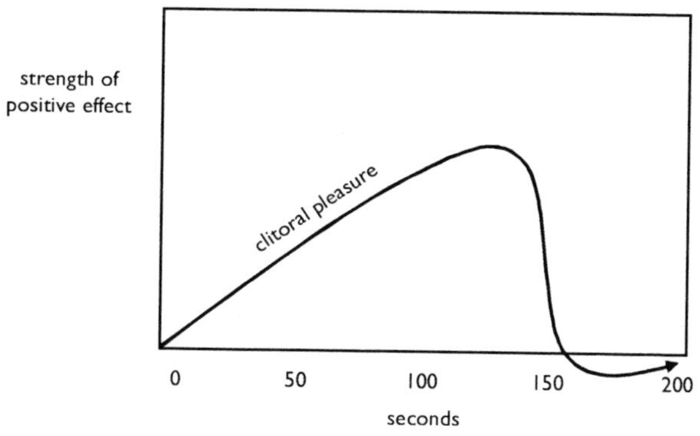

Clitoral pleasure grows stronger with sustained copulatory contact. After clitoral orgasm, clitoral pleasure temporarily becomes a weak negative effect.

CHAPTER 37

CLITORAL ORGASM

Type of Emotion:	sensory reward
Sensory Trigger:	total pleasure threshold is reached
Mental Effect:	positive
Key Feature:	functions like penile orgasm, but weaker effect
Physical Effects:	ejaculatory reflex, erection termination, lethargy

Purpose

Clitoral orgasm serves no purpose. The clitoris, clitoral pleasure and clitoral orgasm are all embryonic leftovers.

Sensory Trigger

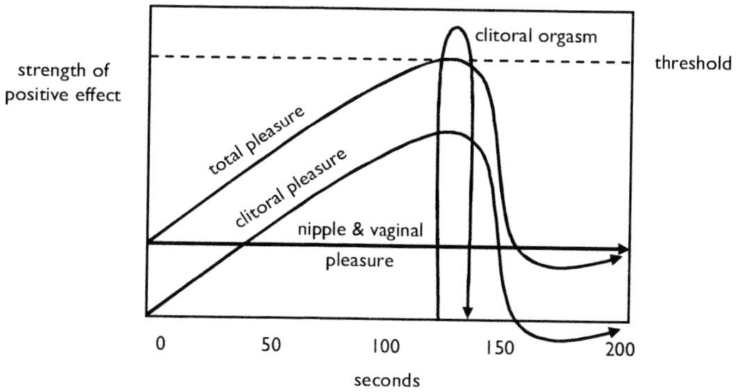

Clitoral orgasm is triggered when total pleasure reaches a threshold. Total pleasure is the combined strength of clitoral pleasure, nipple pleasure and vaginal pleasure.

At least 120 seconds of clitoral pleasure is required to reach the orgasm threshold. Clitoral orgasm lasts 6 seconds.

Chapter 38

Other Types of Sexual Pleasure

There no other types of sexual pleasure.

Sexual pleasure is not triggered by being touched elsewhere. Reproduction only requires contact with the penis, vagina and nipples. Consequently, sexual pleasure is only triggered by contact with the penis, vagina, nipples or their embryonic leftovers. You do not feel sexual pleasure when you are kissed, hugged or massaged. You may feel imagined sexual pleasure if you expect more to follow.

Sexual pleasure is not triggered by touching others. Reproduction does not require touching others. Men mistakenly believe they enjoy touching breasts because they enjoy looking at them so much. Similarly, we mistakenly believe that we enjoy eating because we enjoy the taste and odor of food.

Chapter 39

Lust

Type of Emotion:	sensory coercion
Sensory Trigger:	absence of penile orgasm
Mental Effect:	negative
Sensory Stop:	penile orgasm
Key Feature:	effect grows stronger with time

Purpose

Lust encourages men to copulate.

Lust provides additional motivation to mate, but only when necessary. Sexual pleasure always encourages men to mate. Lust also encourages men to mate, but only when they have not mated recently. The alternative to temporary lust is permanently stronger sexual pleasure, which would cause men to mate too much. Sex would always be better than eating.

Female lust did not evolve. Female lust did not evolve because male lust did. Only one gender needs to seek the other for mating to occur.

Women do not commit crimes or spend money to stop lust. Women do not rape. Women do not need to be told no. Women are not regular customers of prostitutes or strip clubs. Women do not accumulate large collections of pornographic magazines.

Women do desire infatuation. Women's desire to feel this strong positive effect is mistakenly believed to be female lust.

Sensory Trigger

Lust is triggered by the absence of penile orgasm. Ideally, lust would be triggered by the absence of copulation. Unfortunately, men cannot detect the difference between copulation and other methods of achieving penile orgasm.

Mental Effect

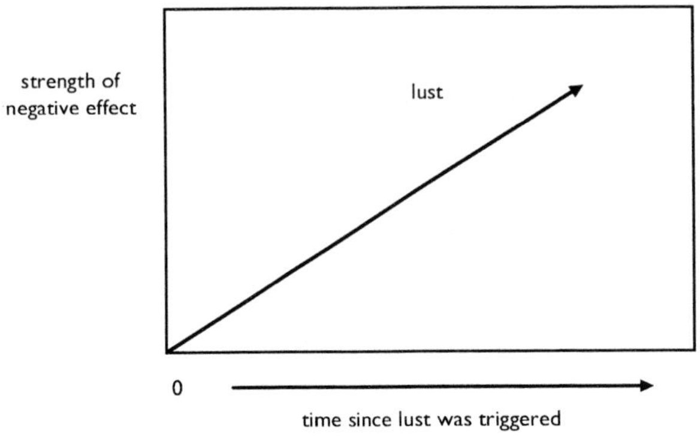

Lust varies with time. The longer a man has felt lust, the stronger the negative effect.

Lust grows stronger as necessary to ensure mating. As lust grows stronger, men are more motivated to overcome obstacles to mating.

Sensory Stop

Lust is stopped by penile orgasm.

CHAPTER 40

REPUGNANCE

Type of Emotion:	sensory punishment
Sensory Trigger:	sexual pleasure triggered by women a man lived with prior to age 6 years
Mental Effect:	negative
Key Feature:	the stronger the pleasure, the stronger the effect

Purpose

Repugnance encourages men to avoid incest.

Female repugnance did not evolve. Female repugnance did not evolve because male repugnance did. Only one gender needs to leave to avoid incest.

The gender difference can be seen when siblings start dating. Boys are uncomfortable when other boys date their sisters. Girls are not uncomfortable when other girls date their brothers.

Sensory Trigger

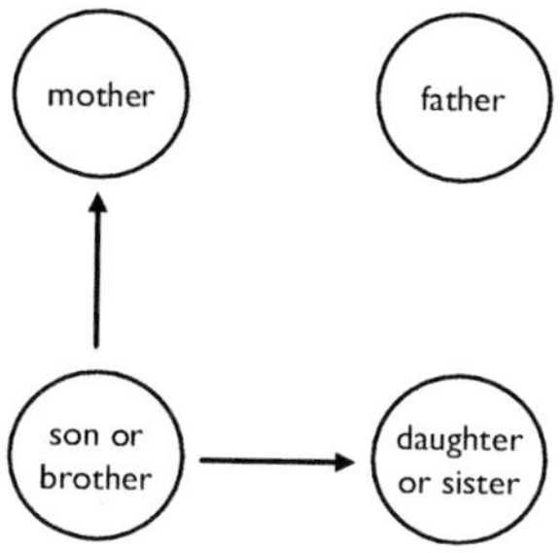

Repugnance is triggered when men feel sexual pleasure triggered by women they lived with prior to age 6 years. Simply put, men feel repugnance when they imagine their mother or sister naked.

Prior to age 6 is a proxy for kin. Prior to age 6, boys primarily interact with siblings. After age 6, they begin interacting with non-siblings. Schooling usually starts at age 6.

This negative sexual imprinting was first suggested by Edward Westermark who noted the "remarkable lack of erotic feelings between people who have been living closely together since childhood". Robin Fox found supporting evidence in Israeli kibbutzim. Unrelated toddlers raised together in a kibbutz never date or marry, as described in *Sibling Incest (British Journal of Sociology).*

Repugnance is not triggered in fathers. Daughters are not alive when fathers were 0-6 years old.

Repugnance is not triggered in brothers that are 6 or more years older. Younger sisters were not alive when older brothers were 0-6 years old.

Fathers and older brothers were not a problem in the past. Fathers would have moved on to a new woman long before their daughters reached puberty. Older brothers would have left home when they reached puberty.

Repugnance is not triggered by other behaviors, like homosexuality. Incest triggers repugnance because it produces defective offspring. Homosexuality does not produce defective offspring.

Mental Effect

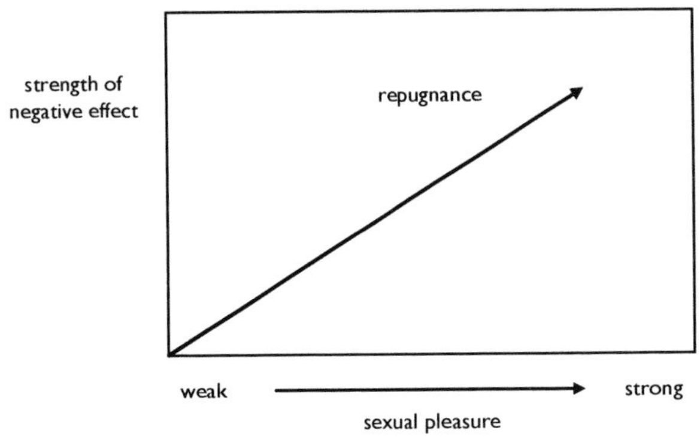

The strength of repugnance varies with the sexual pleasure triggered. The stronger the sexual pleasure, the stronger the negative effect. Men feel weak repugnance if they see their sister wearing tight clothes. They feel stronger repugnance if they see their sister naked. Repugnance increases to discourage the escalation of sexual interest.

CHAPTER 41

AFFECTION

Type of Emotion:	sensory reward
Sensory Triggers:	the visual and audible differences that separate humans from other primates
Mental Effect:	positive
Key Features:	the more incorrect primates excluded, the stronger the effect the more proof of interaction, the stronger the effect the more past interaction, the stronger the effect the more maternal similarity, the stronger the effect the more symmetry, the stronger the effect effect generally stronger in women effect stronger if accompanied by sympathetic behavior
Involuntary Expression:	momentary smiling

Purpose

Affection encourages everyone to interact with kin.

Kin interaction transfers knowledge to future generations. Children learn by observation when they interact with their parents. They learn simple behaviors such as how to eat different types of food. They also learn complex behaviors, such as cooperating for strength-in-numbers.

Kin interaction does not help parents. Kin interaction transfers knowledge from parents to children.

Kin interaction helps children, but they don't know it. Children do not realize the value of learning from parents until they become parents.

Kin interaction preserves knowledge when each generation dies. Current generations use knowledge that has been accumulating since affection evolved. Future generations will also use the knowledge that accumulates between now and then. Current parents teach their children to wear seat belts. Future parents will teach their children to wear seat belts and avoid fatty foods.

Schools are now the primary method of transferring knowledge. Schools provide most of the knowledge downloaded to children. Schools are more efficient than kin interaction. One adult teaches 20 children, allowing 20 mothers to work. Schools also increase labor flexibility. Children are not restricted to learning what their parents know.

Affection also encourages kin to help kin.

Affection gives kin a reason to help kin survive. To maintain the affection that kin trigger, people will help kin more than they would help non-kin. You would rescue your brother from a burning house before you would rescue a stranger. You would loan money to your children before you would loan money to a neighbor.

Affection also helps both genders identify suitable mating partners.

Monogynistic love is not activated without suddenly strong affection. A woman cannot trigger suddenly strong affection in a man unless she is in frequent contact with him. If she is in frequent contact with a man, she would not have time to court or be courted by another man.

Infatuation does not grow stronger and vaginal pleasure is not elevated without suddenly strong affection. If a woman does not feel suddenly strong affection, her man must not feel suddenly strong affection. If he does not feel suddenly strong affection, he must not have fallen in love. Without the proof of love provided by a woman's suddenly strong affection, mating is not encouraged.

<u>Sensory Triggers</u>

Visual affection is triggered by the sight of:

- smiling
- faces with eyebrows, white eyes, chins, everted lips, philtra, down-facing nostrils
- hands with opposable thumbs
- walking that is bipedal
- bums without tails
- feet without opposable toes

Audible affection is triggered by the sound of a human voice talking, laughing or singing.

Affection can also be triggered by stimuli that are recorded or transmitted. Visual affection can be triggered by photographs and video. Audible affection can be triggered by voicemails and telephone calls.

Affection can also be triggered by remembering stimuli. Reading a letter from a friend triggers affection because it causes you to recall memories of the friend's face and voice.

Affection is mistakenly triggered by humanoid faces and sounds, like pets and music.

Affection could not be self-triggered in the past. Before mirrors, you could not see yourself. Before tape recorders, you could not hear your external voice. While you can hear your internal voice, it does not trigger affection. That particular sound is an affection dead-spot.

Affection can be triggered 3 months after birth. Affection can be triggered when somebody becomes familiar. Involuntary smiling, which is triggered by affection, begins at 3 months when newborns see or hear their mother.

Mental Effect

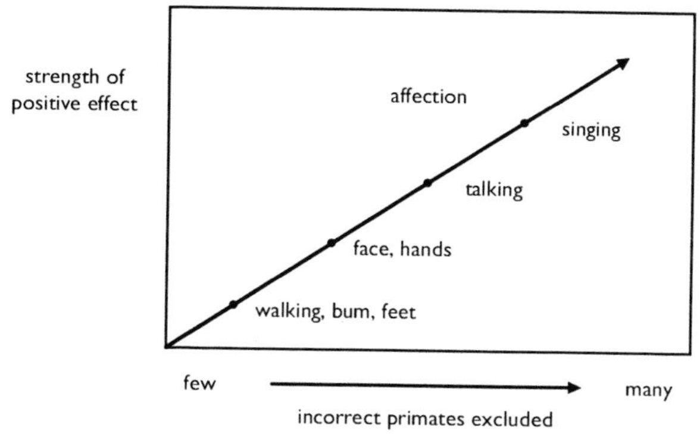

Affection varies with the incorrect primates excluded. The more incorrect primates were excluded by a feature in the past, the stronger the positive effect it triggers today.

	types of primates excluded				humans
	arboreal	terrestrial	partially-aquatic	fully-aquatic small-brain	fully-aquatic large-brain
singing	X	X	X	X	
talking	X	X	X		
face, hands	X	X			
walking, bums, feet	X				

Incorrect primates were arboreal, terrestrial, partially-aquatic and fully-aquatic/small-brain. Humans were fully-aquatic/large-brain primates.

Walking, bums and feet excluded arboreal primates. Only terrestrial and aquatic primates can walk bipedally. Only terrestrial and aquatic primates lost their tails and opposable toes.

Faces and hands excluded arboreal and terrestrial primates. Only aquatic primates have eyebrows, white eyes and chins, which they used to communicate underwater with facial expressions like horror and frowning. Only aquatic primates have everted lips, philtra and down-facing nostrils, which prevented water from flooding into their lungs. Only aquatic primates have opposable thumbs, which they used to open shellfish.

Talking excluded arboreal, terrestrial and partially-aquatic primates. Only fully-aquatic primates evolved the advanced breathing control which also produces human speech.

Singing excluded arboreal, terrestrial, partially-aquatic and fully-aquatic/small-brain primates. The only primates with the intelligence and advanced breathing control required to produce a logical sequencing of continuous vocalizations with the acoustics of a human voice were fully-aquatic/large-brain primates.

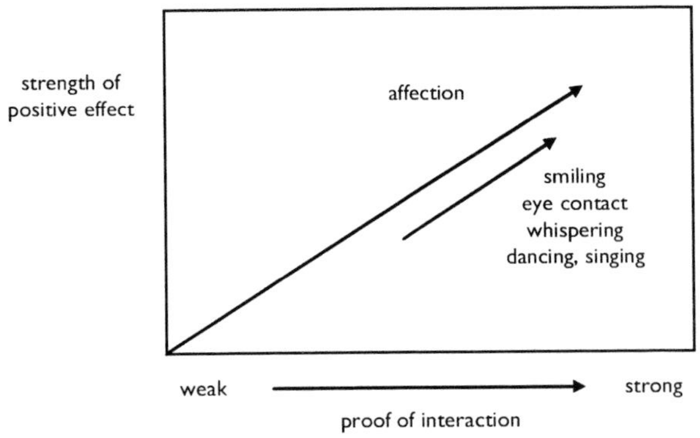

Affection also varies with proof of interaction. The more a feature proves you are interacting with the other person, the stronger the positive effect.

A smiling face triggers stronger affection than a relaxed face. Smiling people feel affection. If you trigger someone's affection, they must be looking at or listening to you.

Eye contact triggers stronger affection than eyes looking elsewhere. Our unique white eyes make it easy to see that someone is looking at you. If someone is looking at you, that person must be interacting with you.

Whispering in somebody's ear triggers stronger affection than normal conversation. To hear a whisper, you must be very close to the whisperer.

Sympathetic behavior triggers stronger affection than passive behavior. Dancing or singing to music triggers stronger affection than just listening to music. Sympathetic behavior confirms interaction with the source of the logical sequencing of sounds.

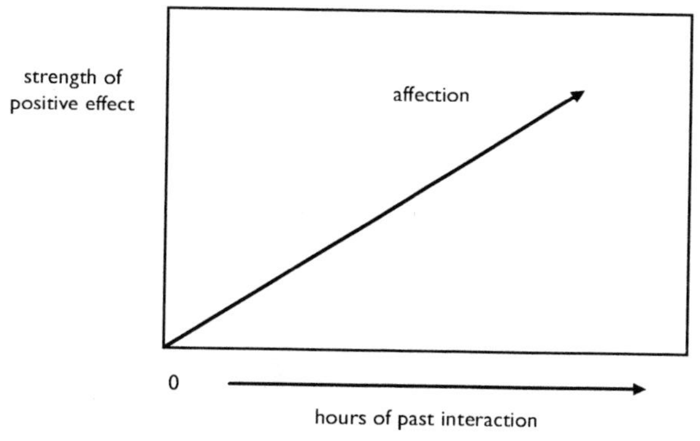

Affection also varies with past interaction. The more you have interacted with somebody, the stronger the positive effect. Kin usually trigger the strongest affection. Early in life, your parents and siblings are the people you have interacted with the most. Later in life, your children become the people you have interacted with the most.

Non-kin can mistakenly trigger strong affection. Spouses, friends and co-workers can easily accumulate as many hours of interacting as kin do. Non-kin triggering of affection helps your group, not your genes. It encourages knowledge transfer between non-kin.

Entertainment stars can also mistakenly trigger strong affection. Oprah Winfrey and Howard Stern have accumulated many hours of interaction with their audiences.

Pets can also mistakenly trigger strong affection. Pets can trigger surprisingly strong affection, given their non-human faces and lack of a voice. They do it by accumulating more hours of interaction per year than humans do. Pets make eye contact with you more frequently than humans do.

Music can also mistakenly trigger strong affection. Like pets, you can accumulate many hours of interaction with a song.

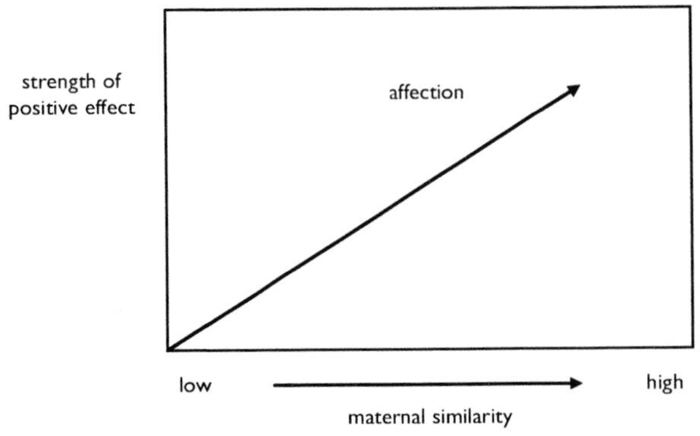

Affection also varies with maternal similarity. The more somebody looks or sounds like your mother, the stronger the positive effect they trigger in you. Looks-like-your-mother refers to visual features that are not gender or age specific, such as eye color, hair color, skin color and facial bone structure. Sounds-like-your-mother also refers to audible features that are not gender or age specific, such as language and accent.

Affection varies with maternal similarity to encourage interacting with kin. The more somebody looks or sounds like your mother, the more likely they are kin.

The effect of maternal similarity can be seen in urban melting pots. People tend to socialize with and marry people who look and sound like them, even when most people around them do not look or sound like them.

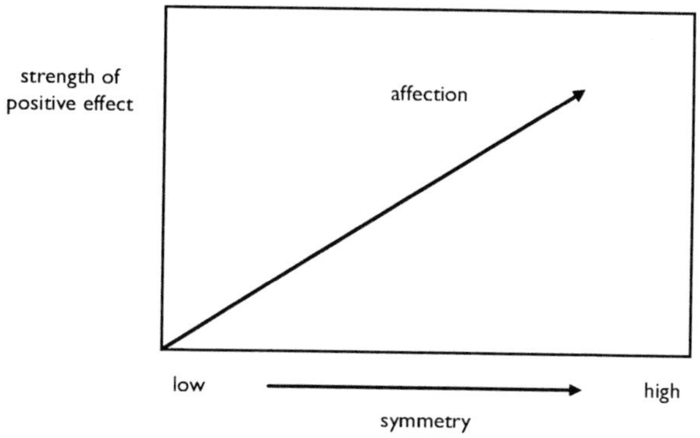

Affection also varies with symmetry. The more symmetrical somebody appears to be, the stronger the positive effect.

The more symmetrical a face appears to be, the stronger the affection it triggers, as reported by Dahlia Zaidel in *Appearance of Symmetry, Beauty, and Health in Human Faces (Brain and Cognition).*

The more symmetrical bipedal movement appears to be, the stronger the affection it triggers. The more symmetrical dancing appears to be, the more people enjoy watching it, as reported by Robert Trivers in *Dance Reveals Symmetry Especially in Young Men (Nature).*

The more symmetrical somebody is, the fewer genetic defects they have. Affection encourages you to prefer interacting with beautiful people. Their genes are more likely to transfer knowledge to future generations.

Affection, cute and loneliness are generally stronger in women. Women enjoy socializing more. Women enjoy infants more. Women dislike being alone more.

Affection, cute and loneliness are stronger in women because they spend more time with children, who are the targets of the knowledge transferred by kin interaction.

Other Species

Cooperative carnivores feel affection. Affection encourages kin interaction to transfer their methods of cooperating to the next generation.

Examples of kin interaction leading to knowledge transfer have been spotted in cooperative carnivores.

Dolphins have been seen using sponges to protect their noses while they scour the ocean floor looking for food. This was reported by Michael Krutzen in *Cultural Tool Use in Bottlenose Dolphins (Proceedings of the National Academy of Sciences).*

Chimpanzees have been seen using sticks to extract termites from trees, as reported by Andrew Whiten in *The Second Inheritance System in Chimpanzees and Humans (Nature).*

Captive killer whales have been seen baiting birds by leaving food floating on the water's surface, then capturing the birds when they land. This was reported in *More Animals Join the Learning Circle (NewScientist).*

In each of these examples, offspring observed and then copied the innovation.

Flags, Currency, Anthems, Politicians & Royalty

Flags, currency, anthems, politicians and royalty are used to promote patriotism, which is national affection.

Flags and currency are poor promoters of patriotism. Because they are ubiquitous, we accumulate many hours of interaction with these national symbols. However, they do not look or sound like humans.

Anthems are better than flags and currency. They are as ubiquitous as flags and currency, but also include a human or humanoid sound. They are also usually accompanied by the sympathetic behavior of singing.

Politicians and royalty are better than anthems, flags and currency. The media makes them ubiquitous and they obviously look and sound like humans.

Royalty are better than politicians. They accumulate interaction longer than politicians. Queen Elizabeth the Second has been accumulating interaction for more than 80 years.

Poetry and Alliteration

We prefer poetry and alliteration for the same reason we prefer singing. They all trigger strong affection because they are a logical sequencing of human vocalizations. ~ *Peter Piper picked a peck of pickled peppers.*

CHAPTER 42

CUTE

Type of Emotion:	sensory reward
Sensory Triggers:	the visual and audible differences that separate newborns from 33 month old children
Mental Effect:	positive
Key Features:	not triggered before 33 months the younger the child, the stronger the effect effect generally stronger in women
Involuntary Expression:	momentary smiling

Purpose

Cute encourages everyone to interact with infantile kin.

Cute encourages infantile interaction because affection does not. Infants do not trigger affection in others. They have not accumulated the past interaction required to trigger affection. Also, they cannot begin accumulating the required past interaction because they cannot talk or walk.

Sensory Triggers

Visual cute is triggered by the sight of:

- smaller scale bodies, face, hands, feet
- relatively larger scale eyes
- clumsy walking

Audible affection is triggered by the sound of a voice with very high pitch and resonance.

Cute is mistakenly triggered by non-kin. You feel cute when you see infants who belong to co-workers or strangers.

Cute is mistakenly triggered by non-human infants, like puppies or kittens.

Cute is mistakenly triggered by scaled-down objects, like the Mini Cooper or Legoland.

Cute is not triggered before 33 months. Infants do not like kittens and toy soldiers, but older children do. Infants cannot transfer knowledge to newborns, but older children can. Older children can help infants learn to speak.

Mental Effect

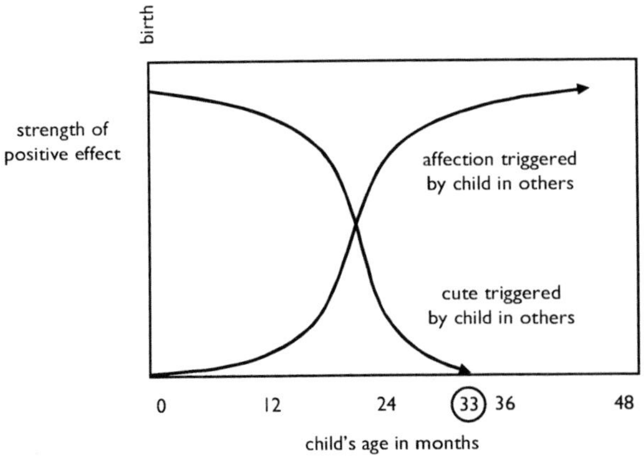

Cute varies with a child's age. The younger the child, the stronger the effect it triggers in others. Newborns trigger the strongest cute. Children that are 33 months or older do not trigger cute. Children stop triggering cute when they can trigger strong affection in others.

The end of cute is the third of four reasons for the terrible-two's.

CHAPTER 43

LONELINESS

Type of Emotion:	sensory coercion
Sensory Trigger:	absence of affection
Mental Effect:	negative
Sensory Stop:	affection
Key Features:	effect grows stronger with time effect generally stronger in women
Involuntary Expression:	crying

Purpose

Loneliness encourages everyone to interact with kin.

Loneliness provides additional motivation to interact with kin, but only when necessary. Affection always encourages you to interact with kin. Loneliness also encourages you to interact with kin, but only when you have not interacted recently. The alternative to temporary loneliness is permanently stronger affection, which would cause too much interaction. Interacting would always be better than sex.

Sensory Trigger

Loneliness is triggered by the absence of affection. You become lonely if you do not interact with people who trigger your affection. Similarly, you become hungry if you do not eat.

Death usually triggers imagined loneliness. If someone dies, you will imagine the absence of their affection in the future. Imagining the absence of their affection triggers your loneliness. The breakup of a marriage or the death of a pet usually causes the same reaction.

Loneliness is usually not triggered until 3 months after birth. Newborns are rarely left alone long enough to feel loneliness. Crying or weeping, an involuntary reflex triggered by loneliness, is usually not seen until 3 months after birth.

Mental Effect

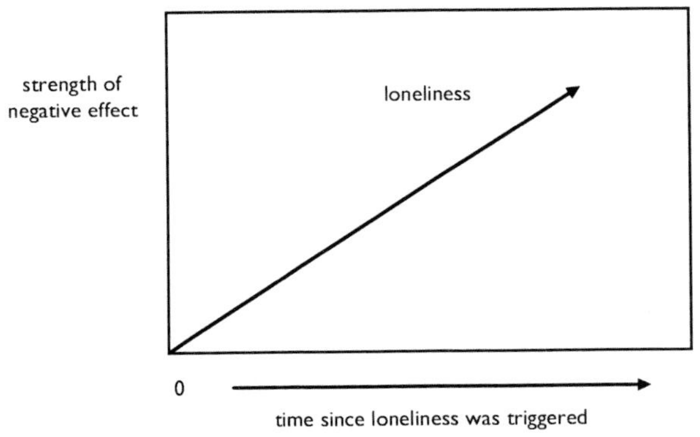

Loneliness varies with time. The longer you have felt loneliness, the stronger the negative effect. After a few months of loneliness, people usually start talking to themselves in a futile effort to trigger their affection and stop their loneliness.

Loneliness grows stronger as necessary to ensure kin interaction. As loneliness grows stronger, you are more motivated to overcome obstacles to interacting with kin. Castaways would rather risk death on poorly-constructed rafts than continue to feel their tortuous loneliness.

Solitary confinement seeks to maximize the strength of loneliness.

Sensory Stop

Loneliness is stopped by affection.

Loneliness is not stopped by interacting with strangers. The widespread loneliness of urbanites proves this. You must interact with people who trigger your affection to stop loneliness. Strangers cannot trigger affection.

Loneliness is not stopped by crying. Only affection stops loneliness. If crying causes someone to interact with you, as it evolved to do, it will indirectly stop loneliness.

People primarily buy pets to stop loneliness, not to trigger affection. They leave their pets when friends call. Pets cannot trigger the affection that a good friend can.

Chapter 44

Excitement

Type of Emotion:	sensory reward
Sensory Trigger:	new scenery
Mental Effect:	positive
Key Features:	the more novel the scenery, the stronger the effect effect generally stronger in men

Purpose

Excitement encourages everyone to explore for new scenery.

Exploring for new scenery helps your group, but harms you and your genes.

Your group has a lot to gain and little to lose. If you find new territory that is habitable, your group headcount can be increased for an infinite number of generations. If you die, you are replaced in one generation.

You and your genes either lose a little or lose a lot. At best, you waste time exploring that could have been used to gather more food or reproduce more. At worst, you die and your reproduction stops.

Sensory Trigger

Excitement is triggered by new scenery. Vacations and weekend trips trigger excitement. The countryside is exciting to urbanites. The city is exciting to farmers. Everyone feels excitement the first time they visit Las Vegas.

Excitement is mistakenly triggered by a change of weather or season. The changing of the leaves and the first snowfall trigger excitement. Christmas decorations also trigger excitement for the first week.

Excitement is also mistakenly triggered by postcards, magazines, television and kaleidoscopes.

Excitement is not triggered by anticipating positive emotions. If someone says they are excited about being promoted, they are anticipating the positive effect of pride.

Curiosity is the desire to trigger excitement. The desire to see what lays around the corner or over the hill is the desire to feel the excitement triggered by a new vista.

Mental Effect

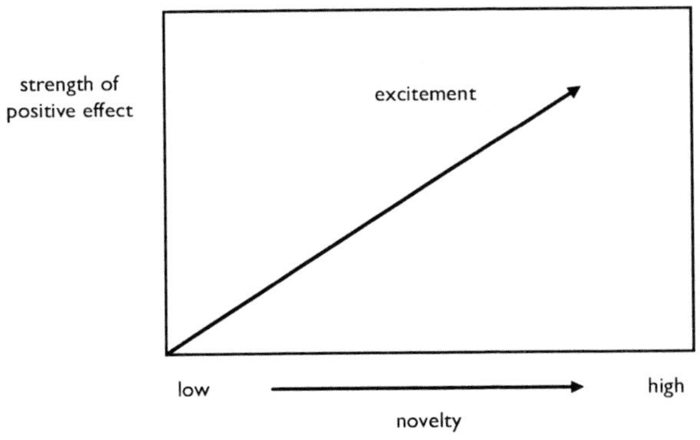

Excitement varies with novelty. The more novel scenery is, the stronger the positive effect. Foreign cities trigger more excitement than domestic cities.

Pleasing Scenery and Excitement

	pleasing scenery	excitement
who	everyone	everyone
sensory trigger	lush scenery	new scenery
mental effect	positive	positive

Pleasing scenery and excitement are similar, but different sensations. Pleasing scenery is triggered by lush scenery, whether it is new or not. Excitement is triggered by new scenery, whether it is lush or not.

Pleasing scenery and excitement serve different purposes. Pleasing scenery encourages living near food. Excitement encourages finding new territory.

The most enjoyable scenery is lush and new, which triggers both sensations.

CHAPTER 45

BOREDOM

Type of Emotion:	sensory coercion
Sensory Trigger:	absence of excitement
Mental Effect:	negative
Sensory Stop:	excitement
Key Features:	effect grows stronger with time effect generally stronger in men

Purpose

Boredom encourages everyone to explore for new scenery.

Boredom provides additional motivation to explore, but only when necessary. Excitement always encourages you to explore. Boredom also encourages you to explore, but only when you have not explored recently. The alternative to temporary boredom is permanently stronger excitement, which would cause too much exploring. Exploring would always be better than sex.

Sensory Trigger

Boredom is triggered by the absence of excitement.

Boredom is not triggered by the absence of any stimulation. Large cities are full of stimulation. Despite this, urbanites become bored.

Mental Effect

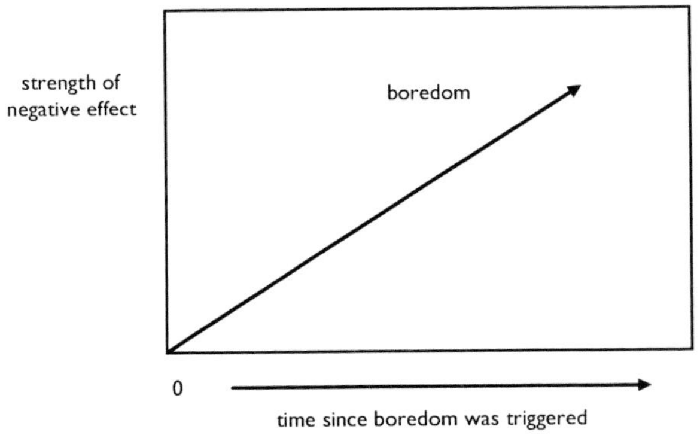

Boredom varies with time. The longer you have been bored, the stronger the negative effect. Boredom is weakest just after returning from your last vacation. Boredom is strongest just before your next vacation.

Boredom grows stronger as necessary to ensure exploring. As boredom grows stronger, you are more motivated to overcome obstacles to exploring.

Solitary confinement also seeks to maximize the strength of boredom.

The scenic sensations are generally stronger in men. Excitement and boredom trigger stronger effects in men than women. Men are more interested in exploring. Men are less likely to sit still for hours.

The scenic sensations are stronger in men because lost male reproduction harms a group less. If a man dies exploring, other men can offset his lost reproduction. If a woman dies exploring, other women cannot gestate more to offset her lost reproduction.

Sensory Stop

Boredom is stopped by excitement. Boredom is stopped by taking a vacation or flipping through a glossy travel magazine.

Boredom can be temporarily masked by other emotions, but not stopped. Boredom does not stop if you start reading a good book. The drama of the book may trigger emotions that temporarily mask your boredom, but it returns when you stop reading.

Chapter 46
Reflexes

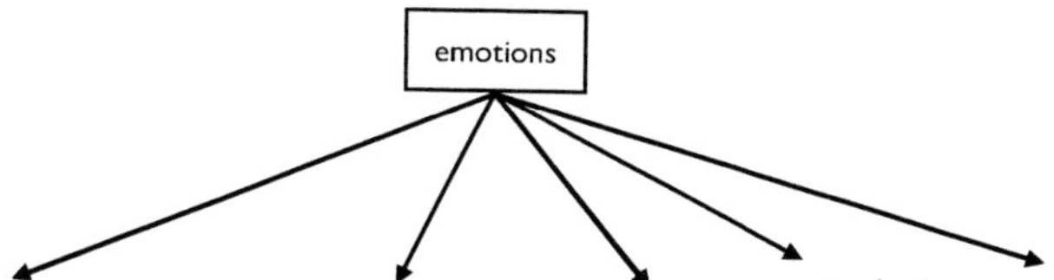

	conceptions	sensations	reflexes	involuntary expressions	voluntary expressions
individual		pleasing taste, hunger, disgust	startle fear		
genetic	maternal love & grief grandmaternal love & grief monogynistic love & grief infatuation, heartbreak jealousy, adulterous guilt	sexual pleasure, lust, repugnance affection, cute, loneliness		horror momentary frowning prolonged frowning momentary smiling crying	
group	revenge, criminal guilt compassion, selfish guilt pride, humiliation humor, envy	excitement, boredom		prolonged smiling blushing	anger laughter

	conceptions	sensations	reflexes	involuntary expressions	voluntary expressions
purpose	direct your behavior	direct your behavior	help you avoid threats	direct behavior of others	direct behavior of others
trigger	conclusions	sensory stimuli	conclusions or sensory stimuli	conception, sensation or reflex	habitual decision
mental effects	positive or negative	positive or negative	suppressive	none	none
physical effects	none	almost none	defensive	facial expressions	facial & vocal expressions

There are two emotional reflexes: startle and fear.

While there are many other reflexes, such as the gag reflex, only startle and fear are generally considered to be emotions.

CHAPTER 47

STARTLE

Type of Emotion:	reflex
Sensory Triggers:	audible, tactile or vestibular stimuli that differs from the past
Conceptual Trigger:	" I detect stimuli than differs from what I expected "
Physical Effects:	arms move up to shield the neck and torso neck and face muscles tense eyelids blink
Mental Effect:	suppressive
Key Feature:	the greater the difference, the more pronounced the effects
Involuntary Expression:	none, although it appears to
Synonym:	surprise

Purpose

Startle helps you survive the initial strike of an ambush predator.

Sensory Trigger

Sensory startle is triggered by stimuli consistent with being ambushed by a predator.

Sensory startle is triggered by sudden differences in what you hear or feel. If you are ambushed by a predator, the audible of the predator's leap will be the first stimuli to reach you. Next will be the tactile feel of the predator making contact with your skin. That will be followed by the motion of your body being propelled forward by the impact, which is detected by the vestibular system in your ear.

Sensory startle is not triggered by sudden differences in what you see. If you see a predator, you can voluntarily prepare. Sudden differences in what you see do trigger the eye blink reflex, which is also triggered by startle. Sudden differences in what you see do not trigger any of startle's other physical effects, like moving your arms to protect yourself.

Tactile, Acoustic and Vestibular Systems Sum to Elicit the Startle Reflex is a University of Toronto study by John Yeomans that explores sensory startle indepth.

Sensory startle can be triggered from birth onwards. A standard test for newborns is making a loud noise to see if their eyelids blink.

Conceptual Trigger

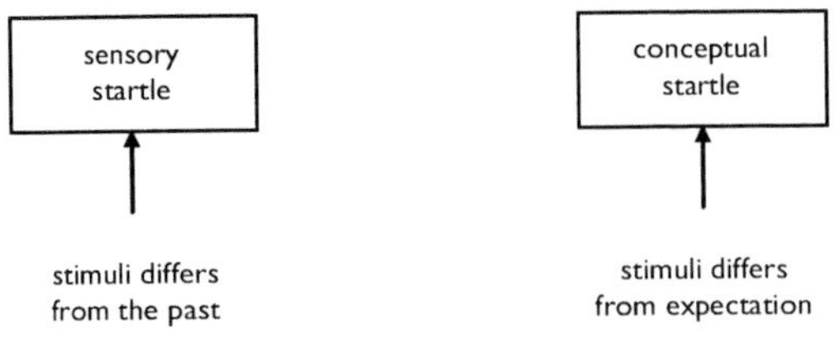

While sensory startle is triggered by stimuli that differs from the past, conceptual startle is triggered by stimuli that differs from expectation. Sensory startle is triggered by a loud noise, whether it was unexpected it or not. Conceptual startle is triggered by an unexpected noise, whether it was loud or not.

Conceptual startle is triggered by any stimuli that differs from what you expected, including what you expected to see. You are startled if you believe you are working alone and look up to see someone quietly standing there.

Conceptual startle cannot be triggered until a child is 24 months old. Prior to this age, children do not imagine the future and therefore do not have expectations.

Physical Effects

Startle's physical effects help you survive an ambush predator's initial strike. Predators pounced on us with claws or plucked us from above with talons. Their initial strikes targeted our head, neck and torso.

Startle causes you to involuntarily move your arms to shield your neck and torso. This prevents the tearing of jugular veins or internal organs. It sacrifices injury to your arms to avoid a fatal injury.

Startle causes you to involuntarily tense your neck and face muscles. Muscles are more difficult to claw through when they are tense.

Startle causes your eyelids to blink. Closing eyelids protects eyes from being scratched or torn out.

The greater the difference in stimuli, the more pronounced the physical effects. Your arms only move slightly if you hear a quiet noise. Your arms move all the way to your neck if you hear a loud noise.

Startle's physical effects save time. You can voluntarily raise your arms to protect your neck and torso. However, deciding to raise your arms loses valuable time. A claw would be through your jugular in the time required to decide to protect yourself.

Mental Effect

Startle triggers a suppressive mental effect. You stop feeling positive and negative mental effects when you are startled. Suppression helps you concentrate on avoiding a threat by eliminating distractions.

Involuntary Expression

Startle does not trigger an involuntary expression, although it appears to. Involuntary tensing of the face and neck muscles looks like a facial expression.

CHAPTER 48

FEAR

Type of Emotion:	reflex
Sensory Triggers:	historic threats and warning expressions
Conceptual Trigger:	" I expect my happiness to change "
Physical Effects:	adrenalin, aldosterone, endorphins released palms and feet sweat piloerection, lip curl bladder and bowel evacuation fainting
Mental Effect:	suppressive
Key Feature:	the greater the threat, the more physical effects are triggered the greater the threat, the stronger the suppressive effect
Involuntary Expressions:	horror, screaming
Synonyms:	terror, anxiety, worry

Purpose

Fear helps you avoid threats.

Sensory Triggers

Sensory fear is triggered by the sight of historic threats, such as snakes or heights.

Sensory fear is also triggered by involuntary warning expressions. You feel fear when you see the expression of horror or hear a blood-curdling scream.

Sensory fear can be triggered from birth onwards.

You can become desensitized to fear's sensory triggers. If you are continually exposed to a threat without being harmed, it stops triggering fear. Most adults do not feel fear when they see a snake.

Desensitizing helps you. If you survive being continually exposed to a threat, it must not be harmful. If reaching a good hunting ground requires climbing a cliff, being continually frightened by the height of the cliff will not help you.

Conceptual Trigger

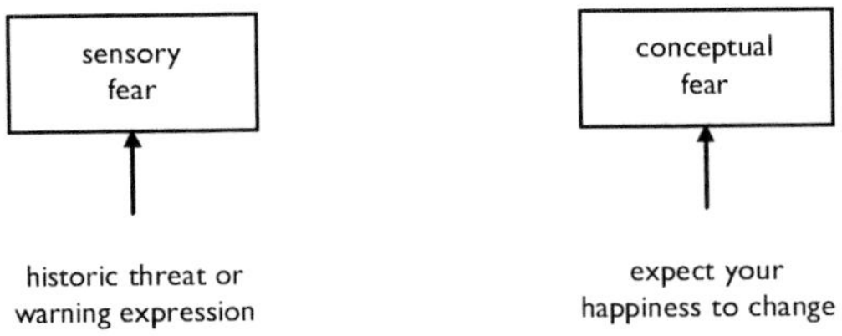

While sensory fear is triggered by a historic threat or warning expression, conceptual fear is triggered when you expect your happiness to change. Bungee jumping triggers both. Sensory fear is triggered by the sight of the distant ground below. Conceptual fear is triggered by the thought of the bungee cord breaking.

Conceptual fear is triggered when you expect any change in your happiness, not just when you expect to feel pain. Your palms sweat before courting a mate or making a speech. Your heart rate increases if you expect to be hired or fired.

Triggering fear when you expect to feel pain is logical. Increased heart rate and sweaty palms help you fight or flee a threat.

Triggering fear when you expect to feel a conceptual coercion may also be logical. The conceptual coercions are jealousy, revenge and compassion. If a woman has committed infidelity, increased heart rate would make a man's anger more credible. If somebody has harmed you by breaking the rules, increased heart rate would make it easier to retaliate. If you see somebody pinned under a machine, increased heart rate would help you save that unfortunate person.

Although it occurs, triggering fear when you expect other emotions is not logical. Fear does not help if you feel love, infatuation, pride or humiliation. Sweaty palms do not help you court the opposite gender or make a speech. Increased heart rate does not help you get hired or avoid being fired.

Conceptual fear cannot be triggered until a child is 24 months old. Children begin to imagine monsters at this age. The onset of fear is the fourth of four reasons for the terrible-two's. The other reasons are: the onset of conceptions, the end of maternal love and the end of cute.

Physical Effects

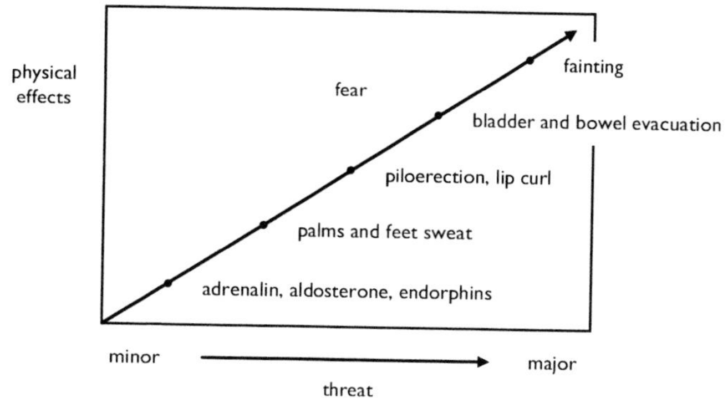

The greater the threat, the more physical effects are triggered. Even weak fear triggers adrenalin release. Only strong fear triggers fainting.

Adrenalin increases your heart rate, which helps you fight or flee an attacker. Aldosterone regulates blood pressure when your heart rate increases. Endorphins suppress pain if you are injured.

Palms and feet sweat to give you better grip. You use the same principal when you lick your finger to turn a page. Fingerprints on your hands and feet also give you better grip.

Piloerection and lip curl make you appear more threatening. Erect body hair makes you appear larger, like a frightened cat. Lip curl shows your teeth. Piloerection and lip curl have almost atrophied since we lost the need for thermal hair and canine teeth.

Bladder and bowel evacuation help fight or flight by making you lighter.

Fainting can evade predation by making you appear lifeless, like opossums do. Fainting is more common in women because it is a better strategy for them. Their smaller size makes them less likely to successfully fight or flee a predator.

Vomiting is not triggered by fear. Vomiting would hinder fight and flight by obstructing vision and breathing. Vomiting is only triggered by survival punishments, like disgust.

Mental Effect

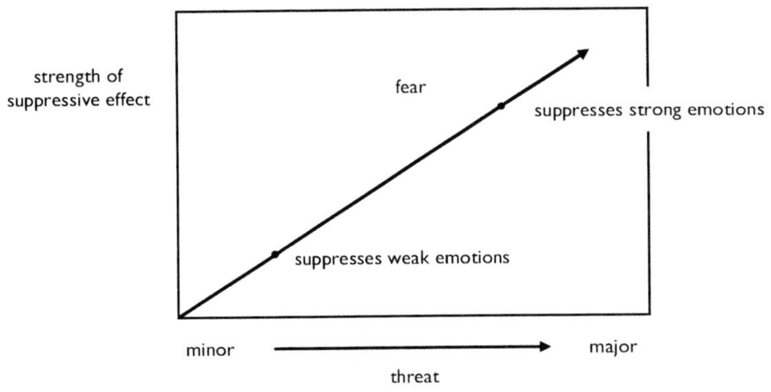

Fear triggers a suppressive mental effect. When frightened, you do not feel positive emotions like pleasing taste or sexual pleasure. You also do not feel negative effects like humiliation or loneliness. Suppression helps you concentrate on avoiding a threat by eliminating distractions.

The greater the threat, the stronger the suppressive effect.

Weak fear only suppresses weak emotions. A horror film can suppress weak boredom, but not moderate hunger.

Strong fear suppresses all emotions. Even strong revenge is suppressed when someone points a loaded gun at you.

People use fear's suppressive mental effect to suppress negative emotions. People enjoy driving fast, taking amusement rides and parachuting because it triggers fear. Triggering fear suppresses their loneliness or boredom.

The placebo effect is the absence of fear's suppressive mental effect. People who do not expect pain, do not feel fear. Consequently, their emotions are not suppressed. They feel better because they can feel positive emotions like affection or excitement.

Fear also triggers better memory storage. You always remember the details of frightening events, like the music that was playing when you were in a car accident. Better memories help you spot and avoid the same circumstances in the future.

Fear does not automatically make you fight or behave aggressively. Your survival is maximized by letting you decide whether fight or flight is better. Automatically committing you to fight would reduce your survival. It would eliminate the option of fleeing, which is usually the least harmful method of avoiding a threat.

Involuntary Expressions

Fear triggers the involuntary expression of horror. While fear evolved to help you avoid a threat, the involuntary expression of horror on your face evolved to help others avoid a threat.

Extreme fear can also trigger involuntary screaming. Involuntary screaming causes serious harm to the screamer by ensuring that attackers know where the screamer is. Because it causes such serious harm to a screamer, it is only triggered by extreme fear. If you feel extreme fear, you are probably going to die. Giving away your location does not cause you additional harm, but it does help save others.

Lie Detectors

Lie detectors detect fear, which is different than detecting lies. Lie detectors detect fear's physical effects: increased heart rate, increased blood pressure and sweaty palms. Fear is triggered if you think you might be caught lying. Fear is also triggered if you think you might be wrongly convicted or embarrassed.

Chapter 49

Involuntary Expressions

emotions

	conceptions	sensations	reflexes	involuntary expressions	voluntary expressions
individual		pleasing taste, hunger, disgust	startle fear		
genetic	maternal love & grief grandmaternal love & grief monogynistic love & grief infatuation, heartbreak jealousy, adulterous guilt	sexual pleasure, lust, repugnance affection, cute, loneliness		horror momentary frowning prolonged frowning momentary smiling crying	
group	revenge, criminal guilt compassion, selfish guilt pride, humiliation humor, envy	excitement, boredom		prolonged smiling blushing	anger laughter
purpose	direct your behavior	direct your behavior	help you avoid threats	direct behavior of others	direct behavior of others
trigger	conclusions	sensory stimuli	conclusions or sensory stimuli	conception, sensation or reflex	habitual decision
mental effects	positive or negative	positive or negative	suppressive	none	none
physical effects	none	almost none	defensive	facial expressions	facial & vocal expressions

fear	→ horror
survival punishments	→ momentary frowning
grief	→ prolonged frowning
affection, cute	→ momentary smiling
loneliness	→ crying
pride	→ prolonged smiling
humiliation	→ blushing

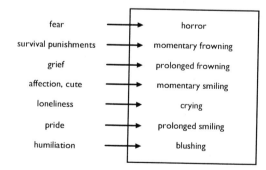

Involuntary expressions are triggered by a conception, sensation or reflex.

	muscular	autonomic
warning	horror	
	momentary frowning	
	prolonged frowning	
social	momentary smiling	crying
rank	prolonged smiling	blushing

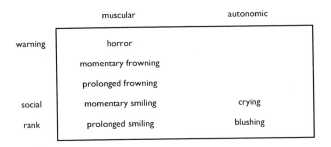

There are two types of involuntary expression: muscular and autonomic.

Muscular expressions use facial muscles. There are three basic muscular expressions: horror, frowning and smiling. Prolonged frowning and prolonged smiling are just extended versions of two basic expressions.

Muscular expressions evolved during our aquatic detour. We used facial expressions to communicate underwater. We are the only primates that smile or frown. We are also the only primates that have eyebrows, white eyes or chins.

Autonomic expressions use autonomic systems. Crying uses the tear glands. Blushing uses the circulatory system.

Autonomic expressions evolved after our aquatic detour. Crying is a re-adaptation of a mechanism previously used to leak salt. Blushing evolved after our three color vision evolved a second time. Three color vision, which is required to see blushing, is only used by terrestrial species.

Involuntary expressions fall into three categories of purpose: warning, social and rank.

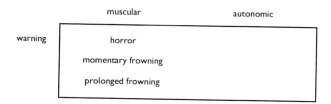

	muscular	autonomic
warning	horror momentary frowning prolonged frowning	

Warning expressions warn kin about harm. Horror warns kin about threats. Momentary frowning warns kin about toxins or trauma. Prolonged frowning warns kin about grief by making it tangible.

	muscular	autonomic
social	momentary smiling	crying

Social expressions encourage kin to interact with you. Momentary smiling triggers affection in kin, which rewards them for interacting with you. Crying triggers compassion in kin, which they stop by interacting with you.

	muscular	autonomic
rank	prolonged smiling	blushing

Rank expressions encourage others to increase their rank or to not reduce yours. Prolonged smiling makes the reward of pride tangible to others. Blushing triggers compassion in others, which they stop by not laughing at you.

Involuntary expressions only help your genes or your group. If an expression helps you, you express it voluntarily.

Chapter 50
Horror

Type of Emotion:	muscular involuntary expression
Trigger Emotion:	fear
Facial Expression:	three circles formed by the eyebrows and mouth eyelids open wide to fully show whites of eyes
Key Feature:	can be triggered at birth

Purpose

Horror helps kin avoid threats. If kin see you express horror, they have extra time to avoid the threat that triggered your fear.

Horror also helps groups. If your co-workers or friends see you express horror, your expression helps non-kin avoid a threat.

Facial Expression

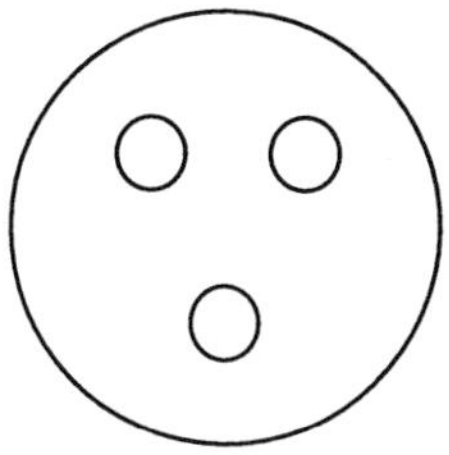

Horror is forming three circles with the eyebrows and mouth. The bottom of the eye sockets form the bottoms of the top circles. Edvard Munch's *The Scream* is an example.

Horror triggers sensory fear in others. You feel slight sensory fear when you look at the diagram above.

Horror is the most visible expression. Horror visibly distorts the face more than the other expressions.

Other Species

Most animals that live in groups have a predator warning expression. Most predator warnings are vocal expressions. Unlike facial expressions, vocal expressions do not require line-of-sight and close proximity. A screaming squirrel warns more squirrels than a squirrel with a horrified look on its face.

Eyebrows

Eyebrows evolved solely for communication. Eyebrows do not protect your eyes. The skeletal bump underneath eyebrows does protect your eyes, but not the hair on it. Eyebrows are equivalent to canine tails.

Only humans have eyebrows, which were used to communicate underwater during our aquatic detour.

Chapter 51

Momentary Frowning

Type of Emotion:	muscular involuntary expression
Trigger Emotions:	survival punishments - bitter, sour, disgust, pain
Facial Expression:	corners of mouth are pulled down
Key Feature:	can be triggered at birth

Purpose

Momentary frowning helps kin avoid toxins and trauma. If kin see you frown while eating or touching something, they will avoid doing the same.

Momentary frowning also helps groups. If your co-workers or friends see you frown, your frowning helps non-kin avoid toxins or trauma.

Facial Expression

Frowning is pulling the corners of the mouth down.

Frowning triggers a sensory punishment in others. You feel a slight negative effect, like disgust, when you look at the diagram above.

Voluntary Frowning

Most frowning is voluntary. We voluntarily frown because it is quicker than saying "my reaction is negative".

Infants often combine voluntary frowning and wailing. Newborns learn that mothers pay attention when they involuntarily frown, so they voluntarily frown to obtain more attention. They also learn that mothers pay more attention when they add the voluntary vocal expression of wailing to their frowning.

Other Species

Only humans frown. Only humans have chins, which prevent frowning muscles from sliding sideways when we frown.

Other terrestrial species stick out their tongues when they detect toxins or trauma, which is more visible than frowning. We would swallow water if we did the same during our aquatic detour.

CHAPTER 52

PROLONGED FROWNING

Type of Emotion:	muscular involuntary expression
Trigger Emotions:	maternal grief, grandmaternal grief, monogynistic grief
Facial Expression:	corners of mouth are pulled down
Key Feature:	longer duration than momentary frowning

Purpose

Prolonged frowning helps prevent the death of kin. Prolonged frowning makes the punishment of grief tangible to kin.

Prolonged frowning also helps groups. If your co-workers or friends see you frown, your frowning makes grief tangible to non-kin.

Prolonged frowning saves more lives than grief. Grief only punishes one person. Prolonged frowning makes grief tangible to many people.

Facial Expression

Prolonged frowning is a longer version of momentary frowning. While momentary frowning lasts less than a second, prolonged frowning lasts more than a second.

Chapter 53

Momentary Smiling

Type of Emotion:	muscular involuntary expression
Trigger Emotions:	affection or cute
Facial Expression:	corners of mouth are pulled up upper eyelids raise slightly to enlarge eyes
Key Features:	can be triggered at 3 months more frequently triggered in women

Purpose

Momentary smiling encourages kin to interact with you. Momentary smiling triggers affection in kin, rewarding them for interacting with you.

Momentary smiling also helps groups. If your co-workers or friends see you smile, your smiling rewards non-kin interaction.

Trigger Emotions

Momentary smiling can be triggered at 3 months. Affection is not triggered until others become familiar. Mothers are the first to become familiar. Children begin involuntary smiling at 3 months when they see or hear their mothers. Blind children also begin involuntary smiling at 3 months when they hear their mother's voice, as reported by Selma Fraiberg in *Insights from the Blind: Comparative Studies of Blind and Sighted Infants.*

Momentary smiling is more frequently triggered in women. Affection and cute are generally stronger in women.

Facial Expression

Smiling is pulling the corners of the mouth up. Smiling is also the slight raising of the upper eyelids to enlarge the eyes.

Smiling triggers affection in others. You feel affection when you look at smiley above.

Voluntary Smiling

Most smiling is voluntary. We voluntarily smile because it is quicker than saying "my reaction is positive". We also voluntarily smile when attempting to trigger affection in others.

Voluntary smiling does not raise the upper eyelid. You can detect this subtle difference. You know that a salesman's voluntary smile is not authentic. His eyes are not "bright and sparkling". This subtle difference was first noticed by Duchene and reported by Charles Darwin in *The Expression of the Emotions in Man and Animals.*

Other Species

Only humans smile.

Cooperative carnivores use vocal or body expressions to reinforce kinship. Cats purr. Wolves howl. Dogs wag their tails. Unlike facial expressions, these expressions do not require line-of-sight and close proximity.

Chapter 54

Crying

Type of Emotion:	autonomic involuntary expression
Trigger Emotion:	loneliness
Facial Expression:	tears
Vocal Expression:	none - wailing is a voluntary vocal expression
Key Features:	frequently suppressed suppressed crying is indirectly released by other emotions not usually triggered until 3 months more frequently triggered in women not more frequently triggered in children
Synonym:	weeping

Purpose

Crying encourages kin to interact with you. Crying triggers compassion in kin, which they stop by interacting with you.

Crying also helps groups. If your co-workers or friends see you cry, your crying encourages non-kin interaction.

Trigger Emotion

Crying is only triggered by loneliness.

Crying is frequently suppressed. Crying is suppressed because it has the stigma of immaturity or instability. Suppressed crying does not go away.

Suppressed crying is indirectly released by other emotions. These emotions cause mental distraction which prevents the continued suppression of crying. That is why people cry when they are with others and therefore not lonely. Tears of joy are the release of suppressed crying by positive emotions like pride or affection. Suppressed crying can also be released by negative emotions, like humiliation or pain, or by reflexes, like fear.

Contagious crying is the release of suppressed crying by the sight of others crying. If you see someone crying, you feel compassion. Your compassion indirectly releases your suppressed crying. Your crying then causes others to feel compassion and to release their suppressed crying and so on. The global cry-a-thon following the death of Princess Diana was a good example.

While crying is a biological adaptation, the suppression of crying is a cultural adaptation. Suppression varies by culture. Men suppress crying more than women. Adults suppress crying more than children.

Crying is usually not triggered until 3 months after birth. Crying cannot be triggered until a child feels loneliness. Newborns are rarely left alone long enough to feel loneliness. Crying is not usually seen until 3 months after birth, as reported by Charles Darwin in *The Expression of the Emotions in Man and Animals.*

Crying is more frequently triggered in women. Loneliness is generally stronger in women.

Crying is not more frequently triggered in children. Loneliness is not generally stronger in children. Children seem to cry more because they suppress less.

Facial Expression

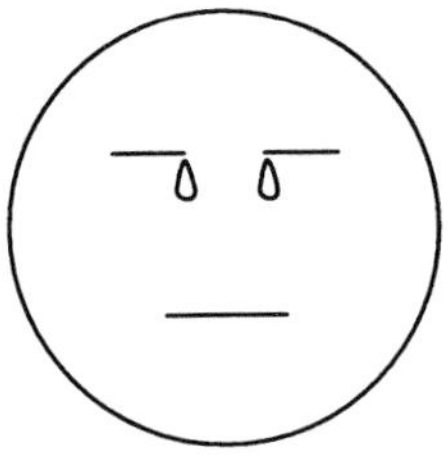

Crying is autonomic because it triggers compassion. If crying could be voluntarily triggered, it would be used fraudulently. All children would cry to obtain attention, whether they were lonely or not. Truly lonely children would not receive attention.

The release of suppressed crying looks like a muscular facial expression. People who are releasing suppressed crying have muscular twitching around their chins that looks like frowning. These twitches are the relaxation of the muscles that suppress crying. Choppy breathing also accompanies the release of suppressed crying for the same reason. Choppy breathing is caused by the relaxing of the diaphragm muscles, which also help suppress crying.

Other Species

Humans are the only primates that use tears to communicate.

A few non-primates also use tears to communicate, as Elaine Morgan reports in *The Scars of Evolution.* Gulls produce copious nasal drippings in confrontations. Sea otters shed tears when frustrated. Both species also use tears to leak salt, which helps their kidneys handle the salinity spikes caused by eating marine seafood.

Chapter 55

Prolonged Smiling

Type of Emotion:	muscular involuntary expression
Trigger Emotion:	pride
Facial Expression:	corners of mouth are pulled up upper eyelids raise slightly to enlarge eyes
Key Features:	not triggered before 24 months more frequently triggered in men longer duration than momentary smiling
Synonym:	beaming

Purpose

Prolonged smiling encourages others to strive for higher rank. Prolonged smiling makes the reward of pride tangible to others.

Prolonged smiling motivates more people than pride. Only a winner feels pride, but many people see a winner's prolonged smiling.

Trigger Emotion

Prolonged smiling is not triggered before 24 months of age. Pride is not triggered before 24 months. Earlier smiling is momentary smiling or voluntary smiling.

Prolonged smiling is more frequently triggered in men. Pride is generally stronger in men.

Facial Expression

Prolonged smiling is a longer version of momentary smiling. While momentary smiling lasts less than a second, prolonged smiling lasts more than a second.

CHAPTER 56

BLUSHING

Type of Emotion:	autonomic involuntary expression
Trigger Emotions:	humiliation stops pride
Facial Expression:	face reddens
Key Features:	not triggered before 24 months more frequently triggered in children and young women

Purpose

Blushing encourages others to mitigate your humiliation during trial-and-error learning.

Humiliation during trial-and-error learning can be permanently demotivating. If you are humiliated during an early attempt at public speaking, you may never try again.

Blushing encourages others not to laugh at you. Your blushing triggers compassion in others, which they stop by not laughing at you.

Trigger Emotions

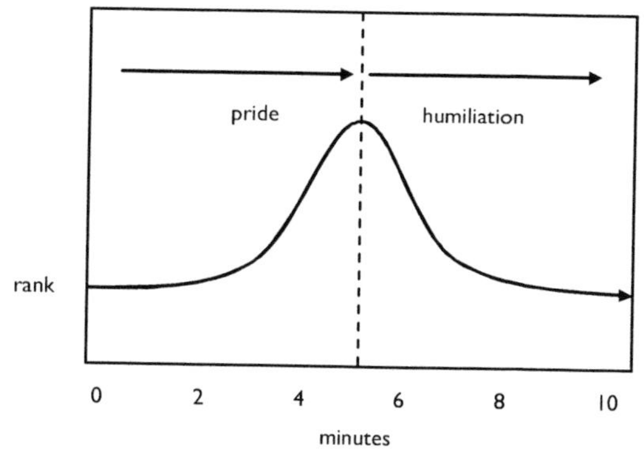

Blushing is triggered when humiliation stops pride. You will blush if you enter a party and everyone looks at your face and then at your crotch, where you notice a stain for the first time. Their attention triggers your pride. The stain triggers your humiliation.

Blushing is not triggered by humiliation alone. You would not blush if you did not notice your stained pants until you had returned home. You would still feel humiliation, but it would not be preceded by pride.

Humiliation stopping pride is a proxy for failure during trial-and-error learning. The rank spike required to produce this combination rarely occurs in other circumstances.

Blushing is not triggered before 24 months of age. Humiliation and pride are not triggered before 24 months.

Blushing is more frequently triggered in children. Children are more likely to experience the rank spikes associated with trial-and-error learning.

Blushing is more frequently triggered in young women. Infatuation makes women more prone to feel rank spikes. Everyone feels pride when a higher-ranking individual treats them like an equal. Young women also feel strong infatuation when a higher-ranking man courts them. The combination of strong pride and strong infatuation makes young women stumble conversationally. Their stumbling triggers their humiliation and stops their pride.

Facial Expression

Blushing is autonomic because it triggers compassion. If blushing could be voluntarily triggered, it would be used fraudulently. People would just blush whenever they made a rank-reducing mistake, instead of taking steps to avoid making the mistake.

CHAPTER 57

VOLUNTARY EXPRESSIONS

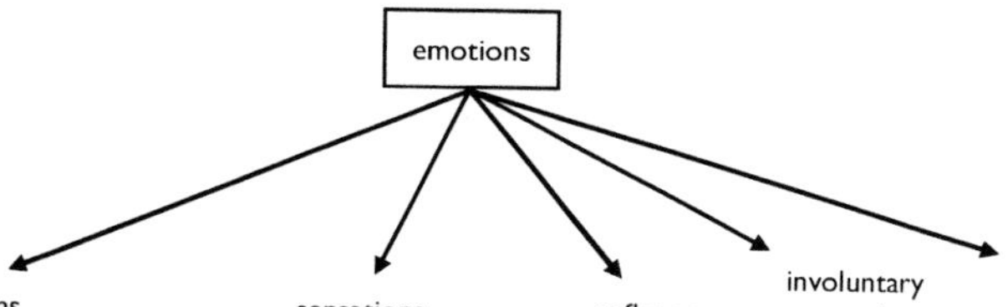

	conceptions	sensations	reflexes	involuntary expressions	voluntary expressions
individual		pleasing taste, hunger, disgust	startle fear		
genetic	maternal love & grief grandmaternal love & grief monogynistic love & grief infatuation, heartbreak jealousy, adulterous guilt	sexual pleasure, lust, repugnance affection, cute, loneliness		horror momentary frowning prolonged frowning momentary smiling crying	
group	revenge, criminal guilt compassion, selfish guilt pride, humiliation humor, envy	excitement, boredom		prolonged smiling blushing	anger laughter
purpose	direct your behavior	direct your behavior	help you avoid threats	direct behavior of others	direct behavior of others
trigger	conclusions	sensory stimuli	conclusions or sensory stimuli	conception, sensation or reflex	habitual decision
mental effects	positive or negative	positive or negative	suppressive	none	none
physical effects	none	almost none	defensive	facial expressions	facial & vocal expressions

There are two emotional voluntary expressions: anger and laughter.

While there are many other voluntary expressions, such as puzzlement, only anger and laughter are generally considered to be emotions.

Chapter 58
Anger

Type of Emotion:	voluntary expression
Preceding Emotions:	usually revenge or jealousy
Facial Expressions:	glaring, flared nostrils, curled lips, clenched jaw
Vocal Expressions:	louder, lower pitch, lower resonance
Verbal Expressions:	profanity, but not putdowns
Synonyms:	rage, tantrum, fury

Purpose

Anger makes threats more credible. An angry threat is more credible than calmly stating "I am being coerced by revenge to harm you". Anger makes revenge and jealousy tangible.

Anger stops revenge and jealousy without physically harming anyone. Credibly threatening someone harms them by triggering their fear.

Anger, like cooperation, is a good idea we learn from others.

Preceding Emotions

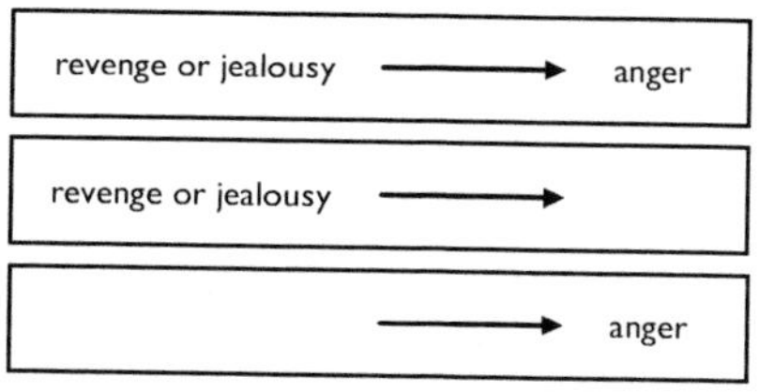

Anger usually follows revenge or jealousy.

Anger does not always follow revenge or jealousy. People rarely express anger when their bosses or the police are present. People rarely express anger when they are alone. If they do, they imagine they are with others.

Anger is not always preceded by revenge or jealousy. Homeowners use anger to deter intruders. Mothers use anger to control children.

Children can express anger as soon as they learn it from others. Prior to 24 months, children just express anger to obtain cooperation from others. After 24 months, children also express anger because they feel revenge. After puberty, men also express anger because they feel jealousy.

Facial Expressions

Anger's facial expressions show your ability to attack. Glaring indicates the completion of visual targeting. Flared nostrils indicate elevated breathing. Curled lips show teeth, our best natural weapons. Clenched jaws highlight muscles that power those weapons.

Vocal Expressions

Anger's vocal expressions suggest masculinity and therefore large size. Vocal expressions are louder, lower pitch and lower resonance. Angry people make nonsensical statements just to yell. Parents often express anger by just dropping the tone of their voice half an octave.

Verbal Expressions

Anger's verbal expressions include profanity, but exclude putdowns.

Profanity is subtle snarling. Profane words show your teeth. Words with hard k's are particularly good for showing teeth. Fuck and cunt are considered more profane than shit and piss, despite triggering less imagined disgust. Fuck and cunt are more profane because they show more teeth.

While profanity is just a threat to harm, putdowns cross the line and cause harm. Putdowns cross the line by triggering somebody's humiliation. Confrontations often escalate from profanity to putdowns to violence.

Other Species

Elephants express anger. After one member of a herd of working elephants was killed by a bus on a highway in Kenya, the remaining elephants began shrieking at the bus and threatening to charge it. The elephants threatened harm, but did not harm anyone. They left when Kenyan Wildlife Service Wardens arrived and fired shots into the air, as reported by *The Daily Telegraph*.

Chapter 59

Laughter

Type of Emotion: voluntary expression

Preceding Emotion: usually humor

Vocal Expression: audible which can be recognized while expressed

Purpose

Laughter is feedback for comedians. It tells comedians they have triggered your humor.

Laughing is better than speaking. Comedians could not understand an audience of people simultaneously saying "I feel humor".

Laughing is better than applauding. Laughing does not require the 1-2 seconds to raise your hands and clap that applauding does. Because laughing is quicker, audiences can use it to provide feedback during a performance without interrupting its timing. Applauding is used at the end of performances, when timing is not interrupted.

Laughing helps establish what is considered low rank. We do not laugh at racial jokes. We do laugh at jokes about racists, like Archie Bunker.

Preceding Emotion

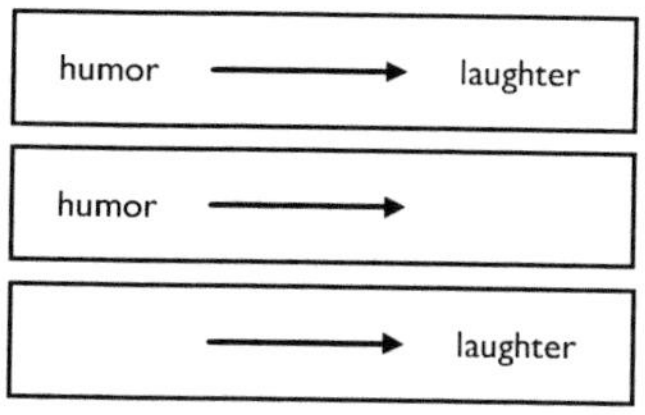

Laughter usually follows humor.

Laughter does not always follow humor. People rarely laugh when they are alone. If they do laugh when they are alone, they imagine they are with others. People who laugh while watching television alone hear the audience laugh track.

Laughter is not always preceded by humor. People laugh at jokes they do not understand to avoid looking stupid. Obsequious employees laugh at their employers' non-humorous jokes.

Children can laugh as soon as they learn it from others. Prior to 24 months, children just laugh to obtain attention. After 24 months, children also laugh because they feel humor.

Seemingly-uncontrolled laughter occurs when your inability to control your laughter lowers your rank. The more you are unable to control your laughter, the more you lower your rank. The more you lower your rank, the more humor it triggers. The more humor it triggers, the more you laugh and so on.

Vocal Expression

Laughter is a sound that can be recognized while expressed. You can recognize other people laughing while you are laughing. This allows a group to quickly provide group feedback. An audience cannot have a meeting and decide what their group opinion is. An audience can listen to others laughing and decide if they want to join in.

Applauding is also a sound that can be recognized while expressed. Laughter is the sound that we agree signals that we feel humor. Applauding is the sound we agree signals that we believe the performance was good.

CHAPTER 60

BEST FOR THE SPECIES

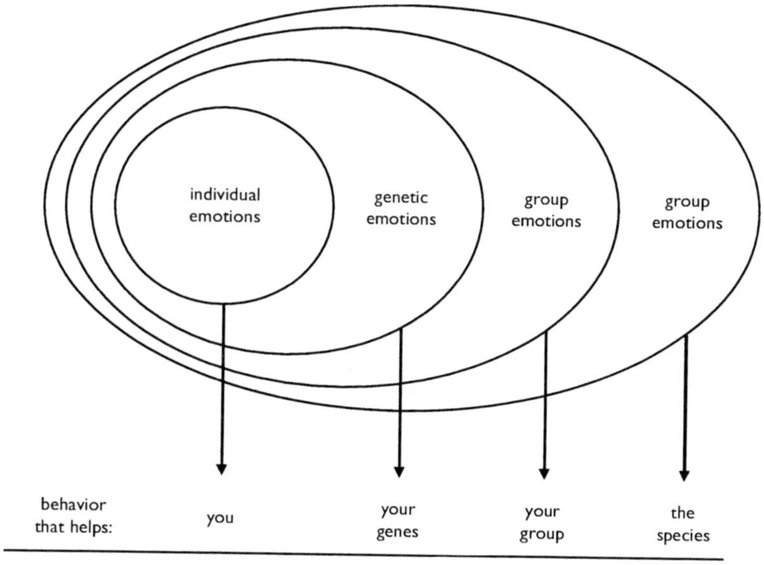

When you maximize your happiness, you do what is best for the species.

Individual emotions encourage behaviors that help you. Those behaviors also help your genes, your group and the species. Eating is an example.

Genetic emotions encourage behaviors that harm you to help your genes. Those behaviors also help your group and the species. Mating is an example.

Group emotions encourage behaviors that harm you and your genes to help your group. Those behaviors also help the species. Increasing your rank is an example.

Group emotions can also encourage behaviors that harm a group to help the species. The race to the moon was an example. The Soviets wanted to feel pride. The Americans wanted to avoid humiliation. Both countries invested enormous resources that could have been used to save the lives of many citizens. Neither country gained advantage over other countries that did not join the lunar club. However, all countries did gain from the accelerated development of aerospace technology. We can now divert asteroids away from earth. It would have been better for the Soviets and Americans to wait for others to make the enormous investment, like the Chinese did.

When you do what is best for the species, you do what maximizes species headcount.

CHAPTER 61

SUMMARY

	rewards	coercions	punishments
post-natal conceptions	maternal love grandmaternal love monogynistic love		maternal grief grandmaternal grief monogynistic grief
courtship conceptions	infatuation		heartbreak
infidelity conceptions		jealousy	adulterous guilt
legal conceptions		revenge	criminal guilt
insurance conceptions		compassion	selfish guilt
rank conceptions	pride humor		humiliation envy
survival sensations	pleasing taste pleasing odor pleasing scenery warmth	hunger, craving, thirst seasonal affective disorder	bitter, sour disgust pain
sexual sensations	visual/audible pleasure penile pleasure penile orgasm vaginal pleasure female nipple pleasure male nipple pleasure clitoral pleasure clitoral orgasm	lust	repugnance
social sensations	affection, cute	loneliness	
scenic sensations	excitement	boredom	

www.theoriginofemotions.com